Gérard
PALOQUE

THE 12TH AND 15TH AIR FORCES

Translated from the French by Alan McKay

Histoire & Collections

12TH AIR FORCE

It was at Bolling Field, Washington, DC, on 20 August 1942, that the 12th Air Force was set up. During the following August and September it was sent to Great Britain and placed under the command of Major-General James H. Doolittle.

Above. **North American B-25 Mitchell, 487th Bomb Squadron (Medium) from the 340th BG (M) of the 12th AF over the Adriatic coast of Yugoslavia in December 1943. The black stains are flak shell impacts, repaired in the field. The American roundels have been repainted over the former British markings whose tail flag is still visible.** (USAF)

Below. **Curtiss P-40F-15-CU (s/n 41-19913) of the 79th FG, Alger-Maison Blanche at the beginning of 1943. In the background, other aircraft types (Hurricanes, Spitfires, Marauders) are clearly visible.** (USAF)

MAKE UP OF THE 12TH AF FIGHTER AND RECONNAISSANCE GROUPS IN 1942		
FIGHTER GROUP	TYPE OF PLANE	TYPES OF PLANE
	NOVEMBRE 1942	DÉCEMBRE 1942
1st FG	P-38	P-38
14th FG	P-38	P-38
31st FG	Spitfire	Spitfire
33rd FG	P-40	P-40
52nd FG	Spitfire	Spitfire
82nd FG	—	P-38
3rd PG (reco)	B-17, F-4, F-5	B-17, F-4, F-5

COMPOSITION DES GROUPES DE BOMBARDIERS (HEAVY, LIGHT ET MEDIUM) 1942		
BOMB GROUP	TYPE OF PLANE	TYPES OF PLANE
	NOVEMBRE 1942	DÉCEMBRE 1942
97th BG (H)	B-17	B-17
301st BG (H)	B-17	B-17
319th BG (M)	B-26	B-26
47th BG (L)	—	A-20
310th BG (M)	—	B-25
17th BG (M)	—	B-26

Surrounded by Flak, B-26B 42-43291 from the 95th Bomb Sq., 17th BG, is dropping its bombs on Ceprano in Italy during the Allied troop landings on the Peninsula in January 1944.
(USAF)

Doolittle had become famous only a few weeks earlier on 18 April 1942 when he carried out the first air raid on Japanese homeland targets, especially the capital, Tokyo, with a group of B-25 Mitchell which had taken off from the aircraft carrier USS Hornet.

In November and December 1943, the 12th AF comprised three transport groups (Troop Carrier Groups) equipped with C-47s: the 60th, 62nd and 64th TCGs. In January 1943, an observation group, the 68th Observation Group was assigned to it, equipped with Douglas A-20 light bombers as well as single seat P-39s, P-38s and P-51s.

The mechanics of this A-36 Apache s/n 42-84207, pose in front of their machine on an Italian airfield. This fighter-bomber, assigned to the 527th Fighter Bomber Squadron of the 86th FBG sports more than 150 mission markings.
(USAF)

Composition de la 12th Air Force à la fin d'octobre 1943				
Fighter Groups	**Bomber Groups**	**Night Fighter Units**	**Photo Reco. Groups**	**Troop Carrier Groups**
1stFG — P-38	2nd BG — B-17	414th NFS — Beaufighter	3rd PRG — B-17, F-4 et F-5	60th TCG — C-47
14th FG — P-38	12th BG — B-25	415th NFS — Beaufighter	68th Obs. Grp — A-20, P-39, P-38 et P-51	61st TCG — C-47
27th FBG — A-36	17th BG — B-26	416th NFS — Beaufighter/Mosquito	-	62nd TCG — C-47
31st FG — Spitfire	47th BG — A-20	417th NFS — Beaufighter	-	64th TCG — C-47
33rd FG — P-40	97th BG — B-17	-	-	313th TCG — C-47
52nd FG — Spitfire	98th BG — B-24	-	-	314th TCG — C-47
57th FG — P-40	99th BG — B-17	-	-	316th TCG — C-47
79th FG — P-40	301st BG — B-17	-	-	-
81st FG — P-39	310th BG — B-25	-	-	-
82nd FG — P-38	319th BG — B-26	-	-	-
86th FG — A-36	320th BG — B-26	-	-	-
324th FG — P-40	321st BG — B-25	-	-	-

Major-General James Harold "Jimmy" Doolittle, photographed in front of a B-26 Marauder at Alger-Maison Blanche in 1943. The hero of the first raid over Tokyo in April 1942 then commanded the 12th AF from September 1942 to March 1943 and then the 15th AF from November 1943 to January 1944.
(USAF)

OPERATIONS IN NORTH AFRICA

The 12th AF was given the task of protecting Operation Torch, the Allied landings in North Africa, which began on 8 November 1942 and so, together with its various units, it set off for North Africa to start operations. The 12th AF then served with the air forces of North-West Africa from February to December 1943 then with the Mediterranean Allied Air Forces (MAAF) until the end of the war.

The 12th AF's fighters shot down 141 enemy aircraft on all fronts but it was actually from a tactical point of view that their contribution was the most significant, destroying as they did enormous quantities of supplies and equipment, interrupting lines of communication, eliminating troop and armour concentrations and destroying railways and rolling stock.

When the 15th AF was created in November 1943, seven Fighter Groups from the 12th AF were gradually assigned to it, the other groups remaining in the 12th AF until the end of the war.

Like the fighters, the 12th AF's bombers gave air support to the British and American troops during Operation Torch, at three different points situated on the Atlantic and Mediterranean coasts of North Africa. Later the 12th AF was reinforced by two medium bomber groups, the 12th and 340th BG coming from the 9th AF.

MAKE UP OF THE 12TH AIR FORCE IN MAY 1945

FIGHTER GROUP	BOMBER GROUP	NIGHT FIGHTER UNIT	PHOTO RECONNAISSANCE	TROUP CARRIER
27th FBG	17th BG	414th NFS	3rd PG	60th TCG
P-47	B-26	Beaufighter	B-17, F-4 et F-5	C-47
57th FG	47th BG	415th NFS	-	62nd TCG
P-47	A-20	Beaufighter	-	C-47
79th FG	310th BG	416th NFS	-	64th TCG
P-47	B-25	Beaufighter et Mosquito	-	C-47
86th FG	320th BG	417th NFS	-	-
P-47	B-26	Beaufighter	-	-
324th FG	321st BG	-	-	-
P-47	B-25	-	-	-
350th	FG340th BG	-	-	-
P-47	B-25	-	-	-

Above. *"Pancho and his Reever Rats"*, this Martin B-26 Marauder (s/n 43-34240) from the 444th BS, 320th BG of the 12th AF, was shot down by flak over Covigliano (Italy) on 23 August 1944. Several planes in this group sported shark's teeth on the fuselage nose. (USAF)

Below. *"Beautiful Baby"*, Boeing B-17F-95-BO Flying Fortress from the 353rd BS of the 301st BG (H) getting ready to take off from Oujda, Algeria on 26 June 1943. (USAF)

January 1945 over Italy, three Mitchell B-25Js from the 340th BG (M), no doubt carrying out a demonstration flight, all the planes having feathered their right-hand propellers. From the rear to the front: s/n43-27661 from the 486th BS (Code 6P), s/n43-2747x from 488th BS (Code 8R) and finally s/n43-27667 "Comin' Over, Hun" from the 489th Bomb Squadron (Code 9Z).

The 15th BS (L) which had had its Douglas Boston IIIs brought over from England, carried out its first sorties from Tebessa airfield less than a week after Operation Torch started. Thanks to the experience it had gathered in the 8th AF in Great Britain, it was a major asset for the 12th AF since the other light bomber groups had no combat experience, even though it only stayed with them for four months

This lack of experience became all too obvious as soon as the groups entered the fray, trying to apply the low altitude bombing techniques they

North American B-25 Mitchell from the 12th AF photographed over the Tyrrhenian Sea, en route for a target located in Italy in January 1945. in the foreground, B-25J-1-NC s/n 43-27661 from the 486th BS in the 340th BG wearing a rather unusual camouflage scheme. (USAF)

The Douglas Havocs of the 12th AF did not only carry out combat missions. Some of them, like this one (an ex-A-20B from the 47th BG) with an unidentified serial number were used for "hunting mosquitoes" in Corsica spreading tonnes of insecticide in the marshes near the 12th AF's airfields. (USAF)

Four Republic P-47D Thunderbolts from the 345th FS of the 350th FG flying over the snow-covered Apennines in Northern Italy. This group carried out ground support missions for US 5th Army troops. (USAF)

had learnt during their training; these had turned out to be effective in the Pacific but they suffered heavy losses when attacking heavily defended airfields, port installations or troop concentrations, causing the 12th AF to change its tactics and carry out its raids from medium to high altitudes.

When the Allies prepared the final assault on the Axis forces to drive them from North Africa, the light and medium bombers of the 12th Air Force joined the fighters and heavy bombers to prevent the Axis troops creating an air bridge and bringing in reinforcements and supplies for the Afrika Korps. The 12th AF also gave air support in the final phases of the African Campaign, sinking several warships and transports and destroying large numbers of German and Italian aircraft both on the ground and in the air. The success of these operations greatly contributed to defeating the Axis powers whose troops finally surrendered on 13 May 1943 in Tunisia.

IN SICILY AND ITALY

The bomber groups later took part in the landings in Sicily (Operation Husky) which started at dawn on 10 July 1943. During the five weeks that followed, the light and medium bombers of the 9th and 12th Air Forces which had been fighting since February 1943 under the unified command of the NAAF (North African Air Force) were constantly involved in attacking tactical targets and airfields.

The landings in Italy started on 3 September 1943 (Operation Baytown) and were preceded by a series of air attacks over the whole of the Peninsula. In order to support these operations,

Although very seriously damaged by AA fire in February 1943, this Spitfire Mark Vb (serial N° ER 210) from the 5th FS of the 52nd FG was put back into flying condition by the group's mechanics. Under its code number you can see the star spangled banner painted onto the machines for Operation "Torch", the Allied landings in North Africa in November 1942. (USAF)

Opposite.
First Lieutenant William J Sloan of the 96th FS, 82nd FG was officially credited with 12 confirmed kills. He is shown here alongside Lockheed P-38F s/n 43-2064 on 13 February 1943.
(USAF)

Below.
A beautiful formation of Douglas C-47 Skytrains in the 12th AF carrying paratroopers taking part in Operation "Anvil" (the landings in Provence). *(USAF)*

THE 12TH AIR FORCE (PILOTS WITH MORE THAN 6 KILLS)		
Name	Group	Nubers of kills
Lt. William J. Sloan	82nd	12
Major Levi R. Chase	33rd	10
F/O Frank D. Hurlbut	82nd	9
Lt. Sylvan Feld	52nd	9
Lt. Louis E. Curdes	82nd	8
Col. William W. Momyer	33rd	8
Lt. Col. Frank A. Hill	31st	7
Lt. Claude R. Kinsey	82nd	7
Lt. Ward A. Kuentzel	82nd	7
Major William L. Leverette	14th	7
Capt. Norman L. McDonald	52nd	7
Major Herbert E. Ross	14th	7
Major Harley C. Vaughn	82nd	7
Lt. Edward T. Waters	82nd	7
La 12th Air Force totalisa 59 as.		

several groups of B-25s were transferred to bases situated in Italy between 24 September and 12 November 1943 and three groups of B-26s were transferred to Sardinia during the same period.

A unit of medium bombers and fighters started operations from Corsica on 10 December 1943. The medium number groups carried out

Below.
Boeing B-17G-30-BO (s/n 42-31855) from the 342 BS in the 97th BG landing on its base on 26 January 1944 after a raid on a ball bearing factory situated at Steyr in Austria. This four-engined plane, which ended its career as a cargo, had its tail damaged during this mission by a rocket fired from a German fighter.
(USAF)

mainly tactical air support missions in Italy, with a series of strikes against airfields situated in Greece, Crete and Rhodes so as to prevent the Luftwaffe from interfering effectively against Allied operations in the Southern Italy, while other groups concentrated their efforts against the railway system by bombing bridges, tunnels and marshalling yards.

From Provence to the Armistice

On 6 June 1944, another front opened up, in Normandy after the Allied landings and in order to prevent the German troops present in northern Italy from heading to this theatre of operations, the 12th Air Force carried on bombing enemy troops and means of transport in northern Italy.

During the preparation of Operations "Anvil"

Above. **No doubt the most famous Mitchell in the 12th Air Force, B-25J-25/27NC s/n 44-30092 wearing on its upper surfaces (in red) the inscription "Finito Benito, next Hiro Hito", together with the emblem of the 12th AF. This twin-engined plan was never assigned to a bomb group and was based at Naples.** *(USAF)*

Left. **Bristol Beaufighter Mk IV F "Fluff/Patsy Amby" (serial number KV 912) from the 416th Night Fighter Squadron seen on its base near Grottaglie (Italy), in November 1943.** *(USAF)*

and "Dragon", the 12th AF undertook to weaken the German defences set up in the south of France and on 15 August 1944 the air forces brought their support directly for the landings in Provence.

During the autumn of 1944, the light bomber groups as well as the fighter-bombers in the 12th Air Force based in Corsica and in Sardinia continued their operations in southern France and northern Italy, moving up the Rhone valley until the German forces in Italy surrendered on 29 April 1945.

Below. **Maintaining a P-38F of the 95th FS of the 82nd FG on an airfield in Algeria at the beginning of 1943.** *(USAF*

2ND BOMB GROUP (HEAVY)

It took part at the end of the Tunisian Campaign then in the landings in Sicily (Operation "Husky") which started in July 1943. Finally it moved to Massicault, then Bizerte in Tunisia.

After carrying out 81 missions with the 12th Air Force, the group was reassigned to the 15th Air Force in November 1943.

The 2nd Bomb Group (Heavy) comprised four squadrons:

— **20th Bomb Squadron** (H), yellow distinctive colour.
— **49th Bomb Squadron** (H), no distinctive colour.
— **96th Bomb Squadron** (H), no distinctive colour.
— **429th Bomb Squadron** (H), no distinctive colour.
(for the tactical symbols see the profiles)

Above. **Marauders from the 319th BG drop their bombs over a target in Italy in 1943. From left to right: B-26B "Mistletoe" s/n 42-96023 from the 439th BS, B-26C "Roger the Dodger" s/n 41-35131 from the 440th BS and B-26C s/n 41-35027 from the 439th BS.** (USAF)

**Boeing B-17F (s/n 42-30082)
du 20th Bomb Squadron (H), 2nd Bomb Group.
Ain M'Lila, Algérie, été 1943.**

230082

Boeing B-17F-75-BO (s/n 42-29907) from 96th Bomb Squadron, 2nd Bomb Group, Massicault, Tunisia, September 1943.

229907

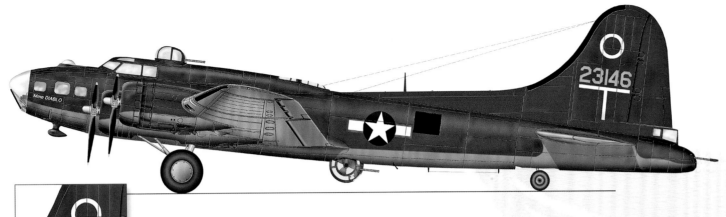

Boeing B-17F (s/n 42-3146) from the 49th Bomb Squadron, 2nd Bomb Group, Bizerte, Tunisia, November 1943.

Tail fin of a Boeing B-17F bearing the markings of the 429th BS, 2nd BG, summer 1943.

12TH BOMBARDMENT GROUP (MEDIUM)

This group of medium bombers was created on 15 January 1941 at McChord Field (Washington) and served in the Mediterranean theatre of operations (MTO)

At the end of 1941, it was changed into a medium bomber group after receiving its B-25Cs. In July and August 1942, the 12th BG (M) sent its Mitchells to Deversoir, Egypt by the South Atlantic route and carried out its first combat missions in North Africa from the following 15 August. Assigned first to the 9th Air Force, it joined the 12th Air Force on 22 August at Gerbini, Sicily. At the beginning of November 1943, the 12th BG (M) started operations over Italian territory, but its days in the Mediterranean theatre of operations were numbered since on 30 January 1944 while based at Gaudo in Italy,

it was reassigned to the 10th Air Force in India and the struggle against the Japanese.

The group was made up of four squadrons:
- **81st Bomb Squadron (M)**, tactical code 1 to 25, no distinctive colour.
- **82nd Bomb Squadron (M)**, tactical code 26 to 51, no distinctive colour.
- **83rd Bomb Squadron (M)**, tactical code 52 to 75, no distinctive colour.
- **434th Bomb Squadron (M)**, tactical code 74 to 99, no distinctive colour.

North American B-25C Mitchell from the 82nd Bomb Squadron, 12th Bomb Group, Gerbini, Sicily, August 1943.

North American B-25 D-10 Mitchell (s/n 41-30344) "Pink Petunia" from the 83rd Bomb Squadron, 12th Bomb Group, Medenine, Tunisia, April 1943.

North American B-25C-1 Mitchell "Desert Vagabond Jnr" from the 83rd Bomb Squadron, 12th Bomb Group, Medenine, Tunisia, April 1943

A group of Mitchells from the 12th BG, over Tunisia in the spring of 1943. In the foreground B-25C "Desert Vagabond Jr." s/n 41-13195 of the 83rd BS bearing a British fin flash. (USAF)

North American B-25H-10 Mitchell (s/n 43-4909) "Eatin' Kitty" from the 82nd Bomb Squadron, 12th Bomb Group, Foggia, Italy, October 1943.

17TH BOMBARDMENT GROUP (MEDIUM)

The 17th Pursuit Group was activated in July 1931, renamed 17th Attack Group in 1935 before becoming a medium bombardment group in 1939 under the designation 17th Bombardment Group (M), equipped with Martin B-26 Marauders.

The group was sent to North Africa via Great Britain and settled at Telergma, Algeria in December 1942 to take part in the Tunisian Campaign. To prepare the Sicily landings, the group bombed Italian bases situated on the islands of Pantelleria and Lampedusa, and then moved its operations to Sicily to support the Allied landings in July 1943.

Based at Djedeida in Tunisia in June 1943 it bombed its targets in Italy then moved to an airfield at Villacidro in Sardinia where it remained from November 1943 to September 1944. The 17th BG (M) took part in the landings at Anzio and Nettuno in Italy in January 1944, then in August of the same year it backed up the landings in Provence.

The 17th BG (M) received its first Distinguished Unit Citation (DUC) during this period for its role in bombing airfields situated round Rome on 13 January 1944.

In mid-September 1944, the group settled at Poretta in Corsica to carry out its missions over Southern France then it was sent to Dijon before joining the 1st Tactical Air Force in November 1944 to support Allied operations in Eastern France and Germany.

It was awarded another DUC for bombing enemy defences at Schweinfurt on 10 April 1945 and was disbanded on the following 26 November.

The 17th Bombardment Group was made up of four squadrons:

- **The 34th Bomb Squadron (M)**, tactical code from 1 to 24 red, red stripes worn on the rear of the fuselage.
- **The 37th Bomb Squadron (M)**, tactical code from 25 to 49 red, red stripe worn on the rear of the fuselage.
- **The 95th Bomb Squadron (M)**, tactical code from 59 to 74 red, red stripe worn on the rear of the fuselage.
- **The 432nd Bomb Squadron (M)**, tactical code from 75 to 99 red, red stripe worn on the rear of the fuselage.

Above. **Martin B-26B-1-MA Marauder (s/n 41-17747) "Earthquake McGoon" of the 37th BS, 17th BG. Partially destroyed by the Flak, this machine made a forced landing at Telergma on 23 March 1943.** *(USAF)*

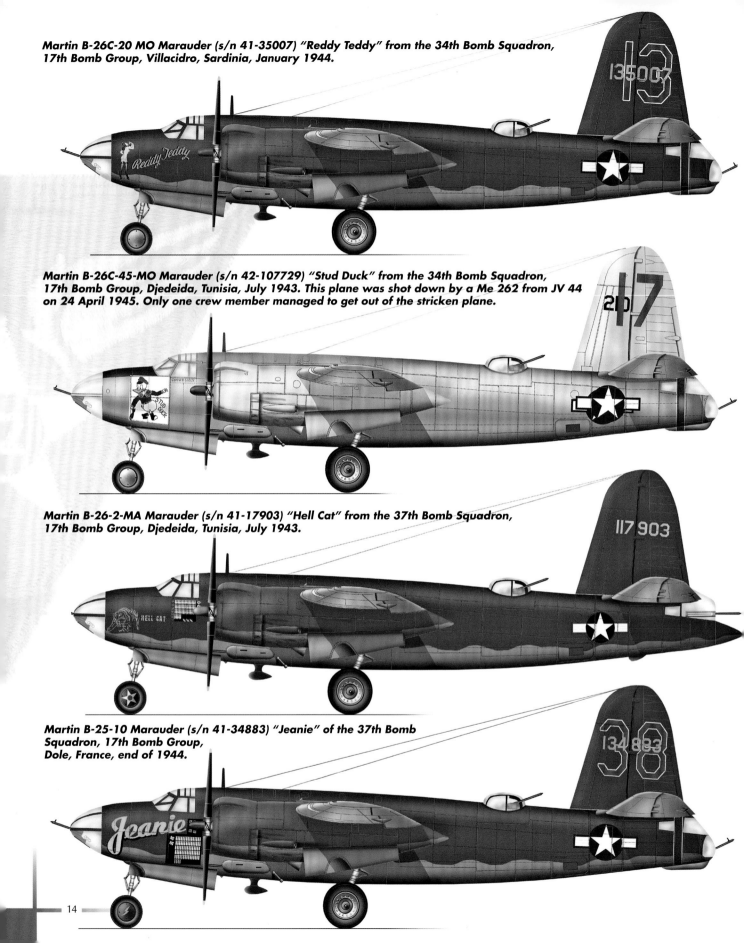

Martin B-26C-20 MO Marauder (s/n 41-35007) "Reddy Teddy" from the 34th Bomb Squadron, 17th Bomb Group, Villacidro, Sardinia, January 1944.

Martin B-26C-45-MO Marauder (s/n 42-107729) "Stud Duck" from the 34th Bomb Squadron, 17th Bomb Group, Djedeida, Tunisia, July 1943. This plane was shot down by a Me 262 from JV 44 on 24 April 1945. Only one crew member managed to get out of the stricken plane.

Martin B-26-2-MA Marauder (s/n 41-17903) "Hell Cat" from the 37th Bomb Squadron, 17th Bomb Group, Djedeida, Tunisia, July 1943.

Martin B-25-10 Marauder (s/n 41-34883) "Jeanie" of the 37th Bomb Squadron, 17th Bomb Group, Dole, France, end of 1944.

47TH BOMBARDMENT GROUP (LIGHT)

This group was formed at McChord Field (Washington) on 15 January 1941. After Pearl Harbor, it carried out anti-submarine patrols along the United States West coast then started training, before being sent to Europe.

It was convoyed by the North Atlantic route in October 1942 then after transiting in Great Britain until November, the group left for Mediouna, Morocco to join the 12th Air Force.

This unit was the only bombardment group in the USAAF to use Douglas A-20 Havocs in the North African and Mediterranean theatres of operations. Its first operations started on 16 December 1942 from Youks-les-Bains, Algeria with the 47th BG very quickly specialising in low-level interdiction and ground support operations. These operations became more and more effective, and during the Battle of Kasserine, Tunisia, in February 1943, the 47th BG (L) was awarded a Distinguished Unit Citation (DUC) for its role in halting the German offensive during this battle. In order to follow the Allied ground troops' advance, the 47th BG (L) moved successively to bases at Thelepte and Souk el Arba in Tunisia on 30 March 1943, the Island of Gozo (Malta) on 21 July, Sicily on 9 August and finally Italy on 24 September.

The group remained there until the end of hostilities on 8 May 1945, except for a period of two months in the summer of 1944 when it operated from Poretta in Corsica supporting Operation "Anvil", the landings in Provence, before moving to Salon-de-Provence, France to support the Allied troops until mid-September as they moved up the Rhone valley.

In January 1945, the 47th BG (L) received a small number of Douglas A-26 Invaders and during the last months of the war, when it was based at Grosseto, it carried out night interdiction missions before carrying out night and day raids from 21 to 24 April 1945, thus perturbing the German retreat along the Po Valley. This was when the group was awarded its second DUC.

Returning to the United States in July 1945, the 47th BG (L) comprised four Bomb Squadrons:

- **84th Bomb Squadron (L)**, tactical code 01 to 24, no distinctive colour.

- **85th Bomb Squadron (L)**, tactical code 25 to 49, no distinctive colour.

- **86th Bomb Squadron (L)**, tactical code 50 to 74, no distinctive colour.

- **97th Bomb Squadron (L)**, tactical code 75 to 99, no distinctive colour.

An A-20, most likely from 47th BG, bombing Cisterna di Littoria, where the German artillery concentrations were a threat to the Allied bridge-head situated to the southwest of Rome. (USAF)

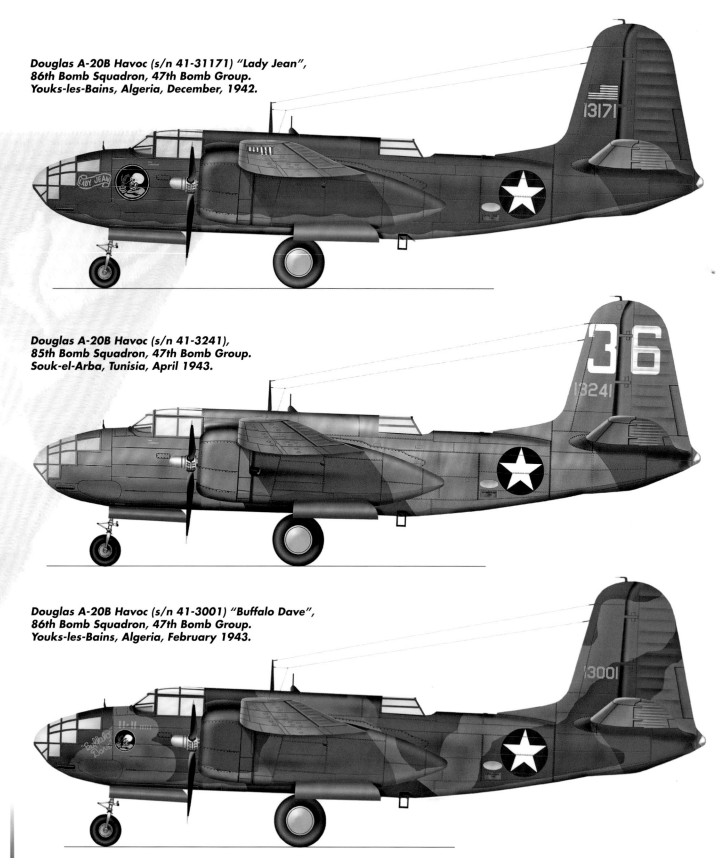

*Douglas A-20B Havoc (s/n 41-31171) "Lady Jean",
86th Bomb Squadron, 47th Bomb Group.
Youks-les-Bains, Algeria, December, 1942.*

*Douglas A-20B Havoc (s/n 41-3241),
85th Bomb Squadron, 47th Bomb Group.
Souk-el-Arba, Tunisia, April 1943.*

*Douglas A-20B Havoc (s/n 41-3001) "Buffalo Dave",
86th Bomb Squadron, 47th Bomb Group.
Youks-les-Bains, Algeria, February 1943.*

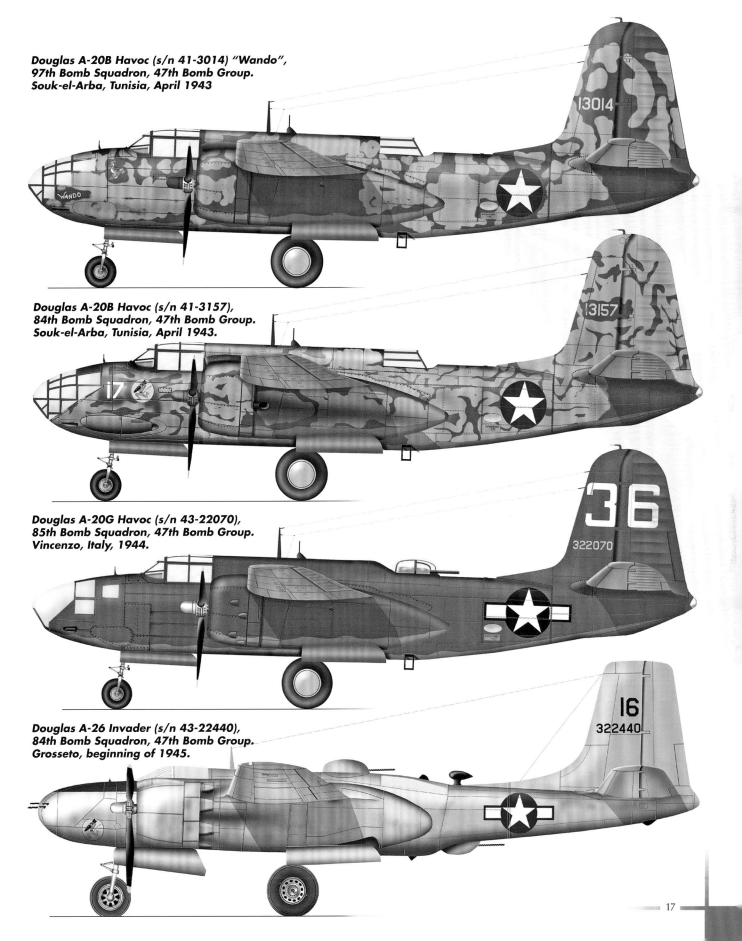

Douglas A-20B Havoc (s/n 41-3014) "Wando",
97th Bomb Squadron, 47th Bomb Group.
Souk-el-Arba, Tunisia, April 1943

Douglas A-20B Havoc (s/n 41-3157),
84th Bomb Squadron, 47th Bomb Group.
Souk-el-Arba, Tunisia, April 1943.

Douglas A-20G Havoc (s/n 43-22070),
85th Bomb Squadron, 47th Bomb Group.
Vincenzo, Italy, 1944.

Douglas A-26 Invader (s/n 43-22440),
84th Bomb Squadron, 47th Bomb Group.
Grosseto, beginning of 1945.

97TH BOMBARDMENT GROUP (HEAVY)

Created on 28 January 1942, the 97th Bombardment Group (Heavy) was activated on the following 3 February and familiarised itself with the B-17 by flying maritime patrols. It was convoyed to Great Britain from May to July 1942 and was assigned to the 8th Air Force. On 17 August it bombed a marshalling yard in Rouen which was the first mission carried out by USAAF heavy bombers based in Great Britain. The group then attacked airfields, marshalling yards, industrial complexes, dockyards and other objectives in France and the Netherlands.

On 13 November 1942 it was sent to the Mediterranean, based at Alger-Maison Blanche, Algeria and assigned to the 12th Air Force. It left Algerian territory on 1 August 1943 to settle at Pont-du-Fahs in Tunisia. In November of the same year, it was transferred to the 15th Air Force.

The 97th Bombardment Group (H) was made up of four squadrons

Above.
This B-17F-5-BO s/n 41-24406 nicknamed "All American", 414th BS, 97th BG collided with a German Bf 109 over Tunis on 1 February 1943 during a mission over Bizerte. Despite the spectacular damage, it managed to return to base and even resumed its mission, after being repaired and transferred to the 353rd BS.

- **340th Bomb Squadron (H)**: a white triangle on the tail meaning the mark of the 97th BG (H) and the tactical code 0. No distinctive colour.

- **341st Bomb Squadron (H)**: a white triangle on the tail meaning the mark of the 97th BG (H) and the tactical code 1. No distinctive colour.

- **342nd Bomb Squadron (H)**: a white triangle on the tail meaning the mark of the 97th BG (H) and the tactical code 2. No distinctive colour.

- **414th Bomb Squadron (H)**: a white triangle on the tail meaning the mark of the 97th BG (H) and the tactical code 4. No distinctive colour.

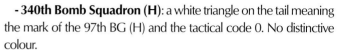

1. Markings for the 340th Bomb Squadron
2. Markings for the 341st Bomb Squadron
3. Markings for the 414th Bomb Squadron

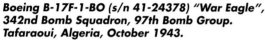

Boeing B-17F-1-BO (s/n 41-24378) "War Eagle", 342nd Bomb Squadron, 97th Bomb Group. Tafaraoui, Algeria, October 1943.

99TH BOMBARDMENT GROUP (H)

It was at Gowan Field, near Boise, Idaho, on 1 June 1942 that the 99th Bombardment Group (H) formed up. It was first issued with four B-17s in October, soon joined by six other Flying Fortresses in order to work on its training.

Assigned to the 12th Air Force, it was sent to North Africa between February and May 1943. It was based at Navarin in Algeria and carried out its first combat mission in March 1943. In order to prevent the Afrika Korps from receiving reinforcements in Tunisia, it bombed German supply ships sent from Italy and Sicily.

On 5 July the group bombed Gerbini airfield, Italy, managing to break through strong opposition from a hundred or so enemy fighters and succeeding in destroying its targets. For this action, the 99th received a Distinguished Unit Citation and carried on with its support missions, particularly during the Sicily landings. In the following August, it moved to Oudna, Tunisia and carried out bombing missions against

1. Markings of the 340th Bomb Squadron - 2. Markings of the 341st Bomb Squadron - 3. Markings of the

Italy. The group was transferred to the 15th Air Force in November 1943.

The 99th Bombardment Group (H) was made up of four squadrons:

- **346th Bomb Squadron (H):** white lozenge representing the mark of the 99th Bombardment Group (H) and tactical code in roman numerals "I"; squadron's distinctive colour: red.

- **347th Bomb Squadron (H):** white lozenge representing the mark of the 99th Bombardment Group (H) and tactical code in roman numerals "II"; squadron's distinctive colour: white.

- **348th Bomb Squadron (H):** white lozenge representing the mark of the 99th Bombardment Group (H) and tactical code in roman numerals "III"; squadron's distinctive colour: yellow.

- **416th Bomb Squadron (H):** white lozenge representing the mark of the 99th Bombardment Group (H) and tactical code in roman numerals "IV"; squadron's distinctive colour: blue.

Boeing B-17F-50-BO (s/n 42-5388) "Never Satisfied", 348th Bomb Squadron, 99th Bomb Group. Tortorella, Italy, March 1944.

301ST BOMBARDMENT GROUP (HEAVY)

The 301st Bombardment Group (Heavy) was created on 28 January 1942 and activated on the following 3 February. After training on B-17s it was assigned to the 8th Air Force with its four-engined aircraft, then left for Great Britain in July and August 1942. It carried out missions over France against submarine bases, airfields and road and railway communication networks.

It left Great Britain in November 1942 for Tafaraoui, Algeria where it joined the 12th Air Force. It was engaged in bombing missions over Sardinia, Sicily and Tunisia and attacked enemy shipping convoys between Sicily and Tunisia.

It was awarded a DUC for its action during an attack on a convoy of merchant ships off Bizerte, Tunisia where it destroyed supplies coming in for the Afrika Korps in Tunisia, flying through intense anti-aircraft fire from the coastal defences and the ships.

In May and June of the same year, still based in Algeria, it attacked artillery positions located on Pantelleria then carried out numerous missions in Italy from July to October.

At the airfield at Oudna, Tunisia, it was transferred to the 15th Air Force in November 1943.

The 301st Bombardment Group (Heavy) was made up of four squadrons:

- **32nd Bomb Squadron (H):** marking of the 301st Bombardment Group (H) represented by a white geometric square shape with the number "1" on the tail. No distinctive colour. Insignia unknown.

- **352nd Bomb Squadron (H):** marking of the 301st Bombardment Group (H) represented by a white geometric square shape with the number "2" on the tail. No distinctive colour. Insignia unknown.

- **353rd Bomb Squadron (H):** marking of the 301st Bombardment Group (H) represented by a white geometric square shape with the number "3" on the tail. No distinctive colour. Insignia unknown.

- **419th Bomb Squadron (H):** marking of the 301st Bombardment Group (H) represented by a white geometric square shape with the number "4" on the tail. No distinctive colour. Insignia unknown.

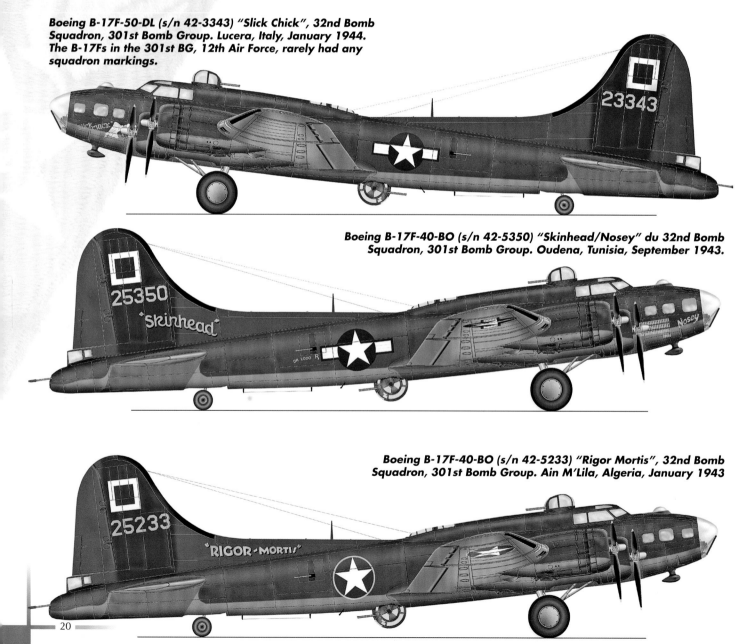

Boeing B-17F-50-DL (s/n 42-3343) "Slick Chick", 32nd Bomb Squadron, 301st Bomb Group. Lucera, Italy, January 1944. The B-17Fs in the 301st BG, 12th Air Force, rarely had any squadron markings.

Boeing B-17F-40-BO (s/n 42-5350) "Skinhead/Nosey" du 32nd Bomb Squadron, 301st Bomb Group. Oudena, Tunisia, September 1943.

Boeing B-17F-40-BO (s/n 42-5233) "Rigor Mortis", 32nd Bomb Squadron, 301st Bomb Group. Ain M'Lila, Algeria, January 1943

310TH BOMBARDMENT GROUP (MEDIUM)

This group, made up on 28 January 1942 and activated on 15 March 1942, was among of the first USAAF groups created in wartime. The 310th BG (M) trained in the United States until 24 September 1942 when it went to England with its B-25s by the North Atlantic route to join the 12thAir Force in October 1942.

On the following 18 November it moved to Mediouna, Morocco and carried out its first bombing raid on 2 December on the port at Sousse in Tunisia. On 21 December 1942, it settled at Telergma, Algeria. Based at Dar-el-Koudia, Tunisia from the beginning of June 1943 onwards, the Mitchells in the 310th BG (M) took an active part in the operations, bombing targets on the islands of Pantelleria and Lampedusa, as well as in Sicily and in Italy.

On 27 August 1943, the group based at Menzel Temime, Tunisia received a Distinguished Unit Citation (DUC) for its effective bombing of the marshalling yards at Benevento in Italy, a raid carried out despite strenuous opposition from enemy fighters, resulting in the loss of three Mitchells and eighteen enemy machines.

On 10 December 1943, the 310th BG (M) was transferred to Ghisonaccia in Corsica where it continued its operations against the German railway networks in Italy. It also carried out missions over Yugoslavia and Austria then in August 1944, it supported ground troops during the Provence landings during Operation "Dragon". It remained based on the airfield at Fano, Italy until the end of the war. On 10 March 1942, it was awarded a second DUC for destroying the railway bridge at Ora, near Bolzano in Northern Italy. The group was deactivated on 12 September 1945 while it was still in based in Italy.

The 310th Bombardment Group (M) was made up of four squadrons:

- **379th Bomb Squadron (M)**: marking of the group shown is that for the middle of 1943 with a horizontal stripe on the fins. At the beginning of 1944 a narrower white stripe was added under it in the colours of the squadron, separated by a black stripe. No tactical code.

- **380th Bomb Squadron (M)**: marking of the group shown is that for the middle of 1943 with a horizontal stripe on the fins. At the beginning of 1944 a narrower light blue stripe was added under it in the colours of the squadron, separated by a black stripe. No tactical code.

- **381st Bomb Squadron (M)**: marking of the group shown is that for the middle of 1943 with a horizontal stripe on the fins. At the beginning of 1944 a narrower yellow stripe was added under it in the colours of the squadron, separated by a black stripe. No tactical code.

- **428th Bomb Squadron (M)**: marking of the group shown is that for the middle of 1943 with a horizontal stripe on the fins. At the beginning of 1944 a narrower red stripe was added under it in the colours of the squadron, separated by a black stripe. No tactical code.

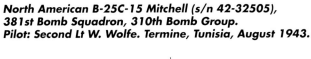

North American B-25C-15 Mitchell (s/n 42-32505),
381st Bomb Squadron, 310th Bomb Group.
Pilot: Second Lt W. Wolfe. Termine, Tunisia, August 1943.

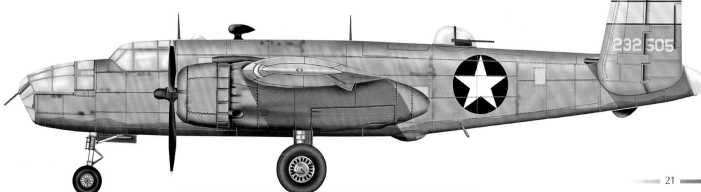

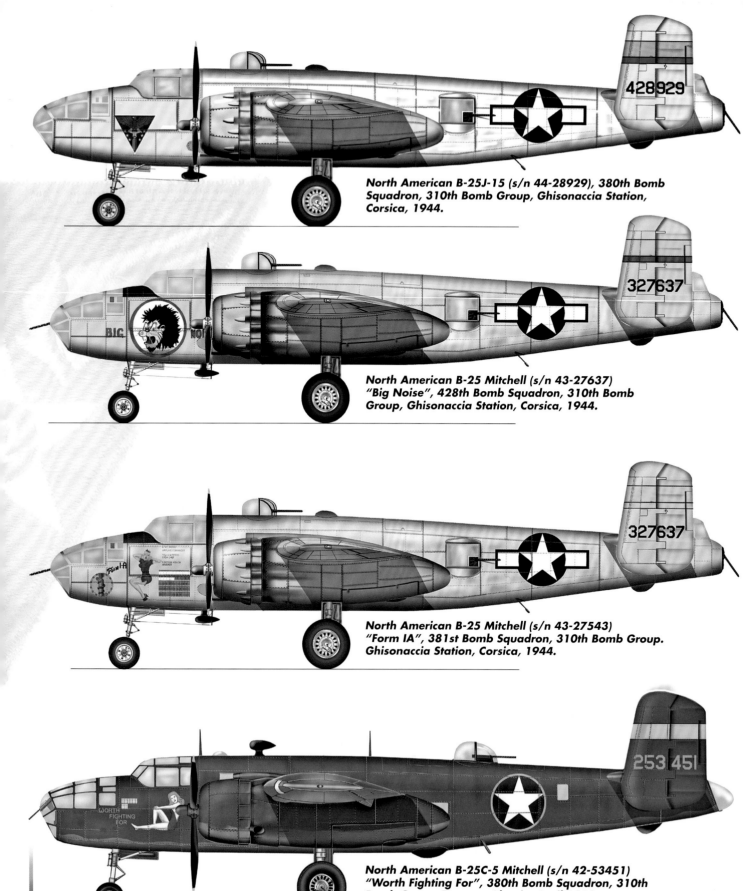

North American B-25J-15 (s/n 44-28929), 380th Bomb Squadron, 310th Bomb Group, Ghisonaccia Station, Corsica, 1944.

North American B-25 Mitchell (s/n 43-27637) "Big Noise", 428th Bomb Squadron, 310th Bomb Group, Ghisonaccia Station, Corsica, 1944.

North American B-25 Mitchell (s/n 43-27543) "Form IA", 381st Bomb Squadron, 310th Bomb Group. Ghisonaccia Station, Corsica, 1944.

North American B-25C-5 Mitchell (s/n 42-53451) "Worth Fighting For", 380th Bomb Squadron, 310th Bomb Group. Berteau, Algeria, April 1943.

319th Bombardment Group (Medium)

The 319th was made up on 19 June 1942 and activated a week later at Barksdale Field in Louisiana. It was equipped at the time with Martin B-26 Marauders. The following August it was training on this type of machine at Harding Field, near Baton Rouge, Louisiana and then in October it was sent to Great Britain by the North Atlantic route to Horsham Saint Faith, where it was assigned to the 12 Air Force. A first detachment from this group was sent to Saint Leu in Algeria on 11 November 1942 to take part in Operation "Torch", the Allied landings in North Africa.

In November 1942, the group was engaged in intensive operations from its Algerian bases but because it suffered heavy losses, the 319th BG was sent to Ouida in Morocco on 27 February 1943 to reorganise. Operations resumed in June of the same year when the group, based in Algeria then in Tunisia, took part in reducing the islands of Pantelleria and Lampedusa and supporting the landings in Sicily and Southern Italy.

From November 1943 to January 1944, the 319th BG was transferred to the 15th Air Force and settled at Decimomannu, Sardinia. In January 1944, it was reassigned to the 12th Air Force, carrying on with interdiction operations in Central Italy and supporting the ground forces during the battles of Anzio, Monte Cassino and Rome.

The 319th BG (M) was awarded two DUCs during the month of March 1944 for missions carried out against railway installations in Rome on 3 March and in Florence on 11 March.

In September 1944, the group moved to Ghisonaccia in Corsica and in October 1944 it started converting to B-25 Mitchells before being sent to the airfield at Seraggia, still in Corsica.

In January 1945, the group was withdrawn from the Mediterranean theatre of operations, returned stateside to convert to A-26s and was finally reassigned to the 7th Air Force which was operating in the Pacific theatre.

The 319th Bombardment Group (M) was composed of:

- **437th Bomb Squadron (M)**: On B-26s: tactical code de 01 to 24. Group's white stripe at the rear of the fuselage, blue stripe with the squadron's colours on the front of the engine cowlings. On B-25s: tactical code de 01 to 24 and tail entirely cobalt blue representing the groups marking. Blue stripe with the colours of the squadron on the front of the engine cowlings.

- **438th Bomb Squadron (M)**: On B-26s: tactical code de 25 to 49. Group's white stripe at the rear of the fuselage, red stripe with the squadron's colours on the front of the engine cowlings. On B-25s: tactical code of 25 to 49. and tail entirely cobalt blue representing the groups marking. Red stripe with the colours of the squadron on the front of the engine cowlings.

- **439th Bomb Squadron (M)**: On B-26s: tactical code of 50 to 74. Group's white stripe at the rear of the fuselage, yellow stripe with the squadron's colours on the front of the engine cowlings. On B-25s: tactical code from 50 to 74 and tail entirely cobalt blue representing the groups marking. Yellow stripe with the colours of the squadron on the front of the engine cowlings.

- **440th Bomb Squadron (M)**: On B-26s: tactical code of 75 to 99. Group's white stripe at the rear of the fuselage White stripe with the squadron's colours on the front of the engine cowlings.

B-25s: tactical code from 75 to 99 and tail entirely cobalt blue representing the groups marking. White stripe with the colours of the squadron on the front of the engine cowlings.

Martin B-26B-10-MA Marauder (s/n 41-18285) « Lady Katy » du 347th Bomb Squadron, 319th Bomb Group. Decimomannu, Sardaigne, avril 1944.

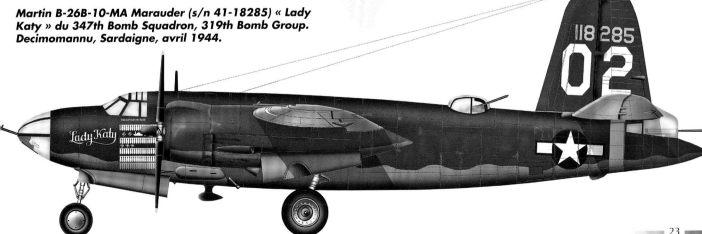

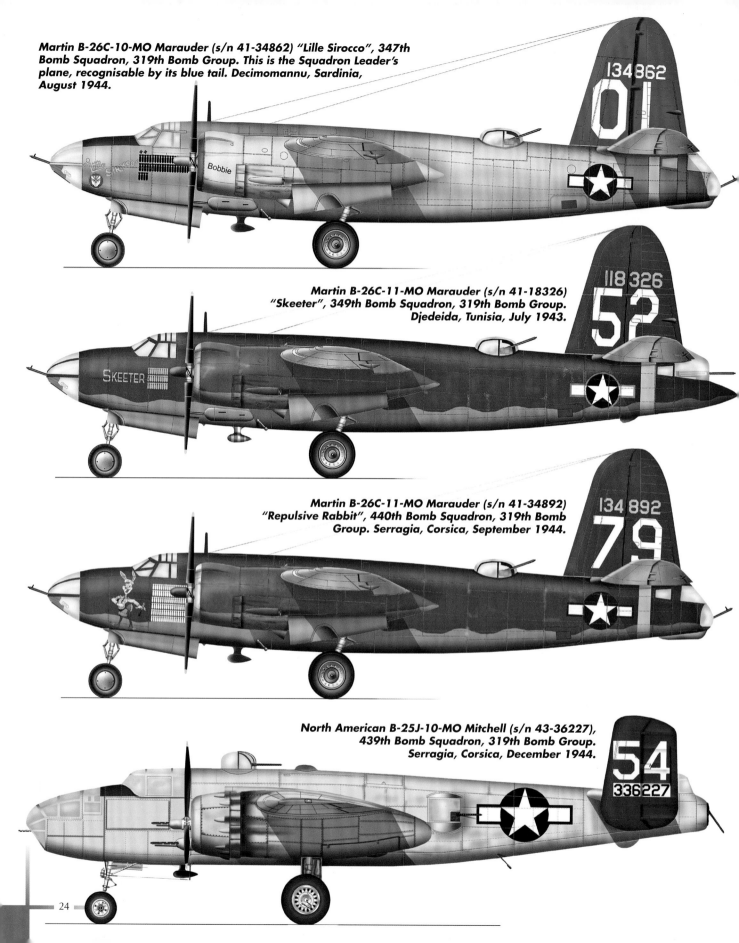

Martin B-26C-10-MO Marauder (s/n 41-34862) "Lille Sirocco", 347th Bomb Squadron, 319th Bomb Group. This is the Squadron Leader's plane, recognisable by its blue tail. Decimomannu, Sardinia, August 1944.

Martin B-26C-11-MO Marauder (s/n 41-18326) "Skeeter", 349th Bomb Squadron, 319th Bomb Group. Djedeida, Tunisia, July 1943.

Martin B-26C-11-MO Marauder (s/n 41-34892) "Repulsive Rabbit", 440th Bomb Squadron, 319th Bomb Group. Serragia, Corsica, September 1944.

North American B-25J-10-MO Mitchell (s/n 43-36227), 439th Bomb Squadron, 319th Bomb Group. Serragia, Corsica, December 1944.

320TH BOMBARDMENT GROUP (MEDIUM)

This group of B-26 Marauders from the 12th Air Force was made up on 19 June 1942 and activated on Mac Dill Field, Florida on 23 June 1942; its four squadrons activated on 1 July 1942. It reached North Africa by air by the South Atlantic route and settled at Oran-la-Senia, Algeria at the beginning of December 1942. It was from Montesquieu, still in Algeria, that it began its combat missions on 22 April 1943, a few weeks before the end of the fighting in Tunisia.

Based at El Bathan in Tunisia from 28 July 1943, the 320th BG concentrated its operations against the airfields and communications networks on Pantelleria and in Sardinia, then in Sicily and Salerno in Italy.

These missions were carried out from bases in Tunisia but after November 1943, the group settled at Decimomannu, Sardinia. In November 1943, the 320th BG was temporarily assigned to the 15th Air Force before going back to the 12th Air Force in January 1944. In the same year it supported the ground forces during the Anzio and Nettuno landings and also during the Battle of Monte Cassino.

Between 18 September and 11 November 1944, the 320th BG (M) operated from its base at Alto, Corsica to support the Franco-American troops moving up the Rhone Valley. On 15 November, it came under the command of the 1st Tactical Air Force, so it could carry out operations from Dijon-Longevic until 1 April 1945; it then moved to Dôle-Tavaux where it remained until the end of the war.

The 320th BG (M) was awarded two DUCs, the first for bombing enemy troop concentrations at Fondi, Italy on 12 May 1944 and the second for destroying fortifications on the Siegfried Line in Germany on 15 March 1945. The group was disbanded stateside on 4 December 1945.

Above. **B-26C Marauder, 442nd BS, 320th BG flying over the Mediterranean coast of Italy during the Anzio landings. In the foreground s/n 41-35179 "Oozin Suzan" and next to it s/n 42-95758 which crashed on take off on 15 August 1944.**
(USAF)

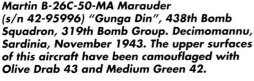

Martin B-26C-50-MA Marauder (s/n 42-95996) "Gunga Din", 438th Bomb Squadron, 319th Bomb Group. Decimomannu, Sardinia, November 1943. The upper surfaces of this aircraft have been camouflaged with Olive Drab 43 and Medium Green 42.

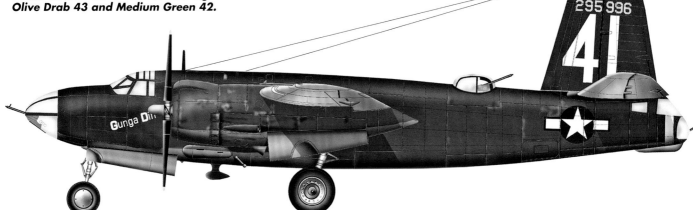

The 320th bombardment Group (M) comprised four squadrons:

- **441st Bomb Squadron (M)**: yellow tactical code from 01 to 24, yellow stripe representing the group on the rear of the fuselage. Red stripe with the colours of the squadron on the front of the engine cowlings.

- **442nd Bomb Squadron (M)**: yellow tactical code from 25 to 49, yellow stripe representing the group on the rear of the fuselage. Red stripe with the colours of the squadron on the front of the engine cowlings.

- **443rd Bomb Squadron (M)**: yellow tactical code from 50 to 74, yellow stripe representing the group on the rear of the fuselage. Red stripe with the colours of the squadron on the front of the engine cowlings

- **444th Bomb Squadron (M)**: yellow tactical code from 75 to 99, yellow stripe representing the group on the rear of the fuselage. Red stripe with the colours of the squadron on the front of the engine cowlings.

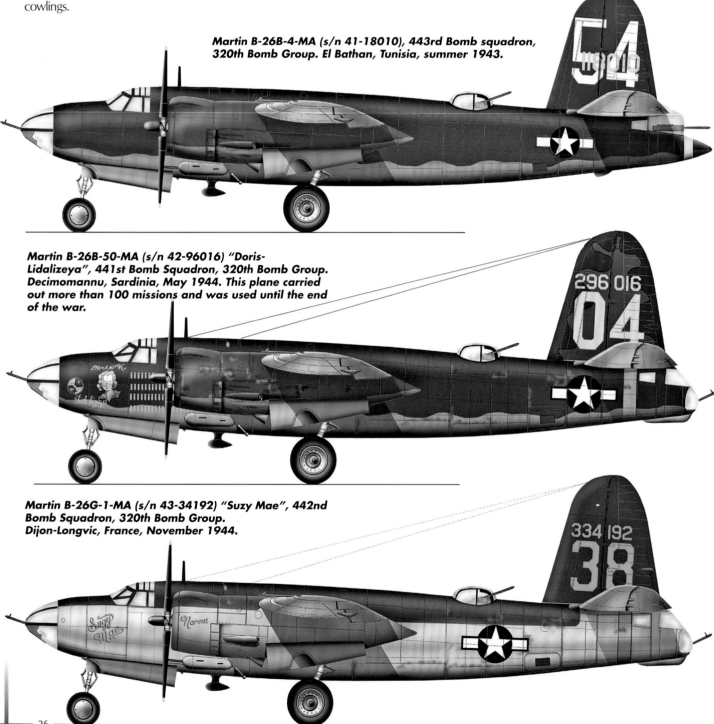

Martin B-26B-4-MA (s/n 41-18010), 443rd Bomb squadron, 320th Bomb Group. El Bathan, Tunisia, summer 1943.

Martin B-26B-50-MA (s/n 42-96016) "Doris-Lidalizeya", 441st Bomb Squadron, 320th Bomb Group. Decimomannu, Sardinia, May 1944. This plane carried out more than 100 missions and was used until the end of the war.

Martin B-26G-1-MA (s/n 43-34192) "Suzy Mae", 442nd Bomb Squadron, 320th Bomb Group. Dijon-Longvic, France, November 1944.

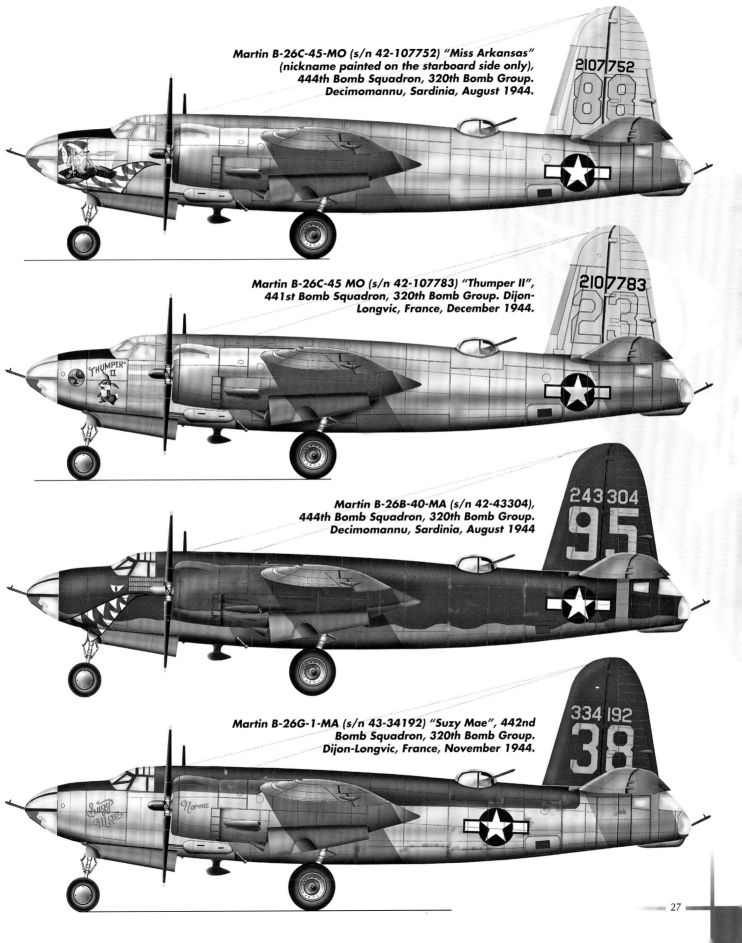

Martin B-26C-45-MO (s/n 42-107752) "Miss Arkansas" (nickname painted on the starboard side only), 444th Bomb Squadron, 320th Bomb Group. Decimomannu, Sardinia, August 1944.

Martin B-26C-45 MO (s/n 42-107783) "Thumper II", 441st Bomb Squadron, 320th Bomb Group. Dijon-Longvic, France, December 1944.

Martin B-26B-40-MA (s/n 42-43304), 444th Bomb Squadron, 320th Bomb Group. Decimomannu, Sardinia, August 1944

Martin B-26G-1-MA (s/n 43-34192) "Suzy Mae", 442nd Bomb Squadron, 320th Bomb Group. Dijon-Longvic, France, November 1944.

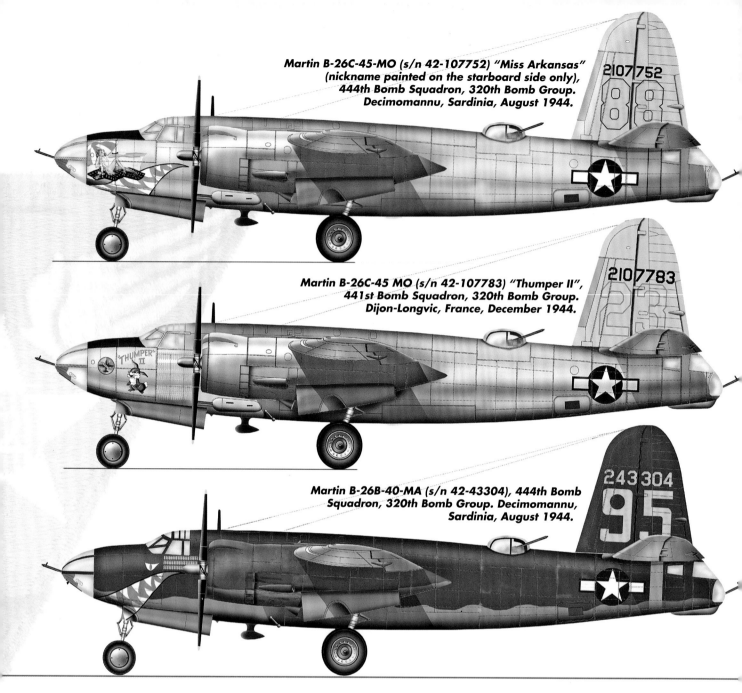

Martin B-26C-45-MO (s/n 42-107752) "Miss Arkansas"
(nickname painted on the starboard side only),
444th Bomb Squadron, 320th Bomb Group.
Decimomannu, Sardinia, August 1944.

Martin B-26C-45 MO (s/n 42-107783) "Thumper II",
441st Bomb Squadron, 320th Bomb Group.
Dijon-Longvic, France, December 1944.

Martin B-26B-40-MA (s/n 42-43304), 444th Bomb
Squadron, 320th Bomb Group. Decimomannu,
Sardinia, August 1944.

321ST BOMBARDMENT GROUP (MEDIUM)

The 321st BG (M) was formed on 19 June 1942 and activated on the 26th of the same month at Barksdale Field, Louisiana. It set off for North Africa with its B-25C Mitchells by the South Atlantic route and settled at Oujda, Morocco on 2 March 1942. Assigned to the 12th Air Force, it moved to Ain M'lila, Algeria on 12 March 1943 before beginning operations on the 15th. It distinguished itself at once by attacking a convoy, sinking seven ships. At the end of the Tunisian campaign, the group moved to Souk-el-Arba, Tunisia on 1 June 1943, continuing its attacks on enemy ships and supporting the landings in Sicily and in Italy.

On 3 October 1943, the group moved to Grottaglie, Italy carrying out a mission five days later against an airfield situated near Athens, which earned it its first DUC.

The 19 February 1944 was a black day for the unit since five of its B-25s were shot down by the Luftwaffe, with three other machines crashing because of bad weather, with a loss of thirty or so men.

It was from its Italian bases as it followed the Allies' progression that it carried out its missions against targets situated in Italy and the Balkans, until 24 April 1944 when it was transferred to Solenzara, Corsica, to carry out operations over Northern Italy and Southern France.

The group was awarded its second DUC on 18 November 1944 for bombing French warships in the port of Toulon, an operation launched to prevent the Germans using the ships. The group remained in Corsica until 1 April 1945 then moved to Falconara, Italy where it remained based until 29 April when the German troops in Italy ceased hostilities. The 321st was finally disbanded on 12 September 1945.

Above. **A formation of B-25 Mitchells of the 321st BG (M) in flight.** *(USAF)*

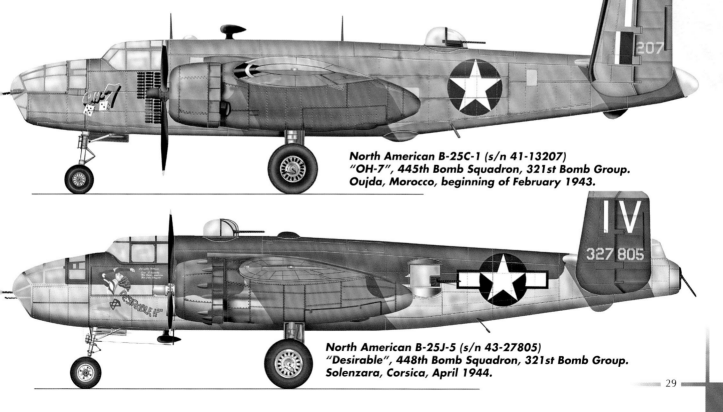

North American B-25C-1 (s/n 41-13207) "OH-7", 445th Bomb Squadron, 321st Bomb Group. Oujda, Morocco, beginning of February 1943.

North American B-25J-5 (s/n 43-27805) "Desirable", 448th Bomb Squadron, 321st Bomb Group. Solenzara, Corsica, April 1944.

The 321st Bombardment Group (M) comprised four squadrons:

- **445th Bomb Squadron (M)**: tactical code from 1943 to January 1945 represented by the Roman numeral "I" on the tailfins and changed between January and May 1945 to a tactical code ranging from 1 to 25. The marking for the 321st BG (M) was represented by a red stripe painted on the top of the tail.

- **446th Bomb Squadron (M)**: tactical code from 1943 to January 1945, represented by the Roman numeral "II" on the tailfins and changed between January and May 1945 to a tactical code ranging from 26 to 50. The marking for the 321st BG (M) was represented by a red stripe painted on the top of the tail.

- **447th Bomb Squadron (M)**: tactical code from 1943 to January 1945, represented by the Roman numeral "III" on the tailfins and changed between January and May 1945 to a tactical code ranging from 51 to 75. The marking for the 321st BG (M) was represented by a red stripe painted on the top of the tail. The marking for the 321st BG (M) was represented by a red stripe painted on the top of the tail.

- **448th Bomb Squadron (M)**: tactical code from 1943 to January 1945, represented by the Roman numeral "IV" on the tailfins and changed between January and May 1945 to a tactical code ranging from 76 to 99. The marking for the 321st BG (M) was represented by a red stripe painted on the top of the tail.

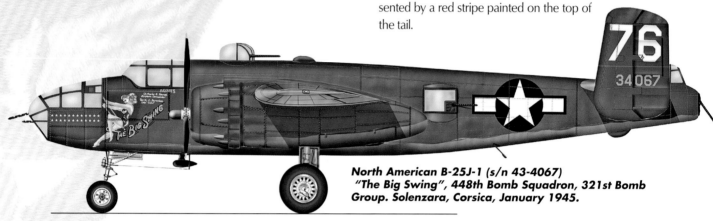

North American B-25J-1 (s/n 43-4067)
"The Big Swing", 448th Bomb Squadron, 321st Bomb Group. Solenzara, Corsica, January 1945.

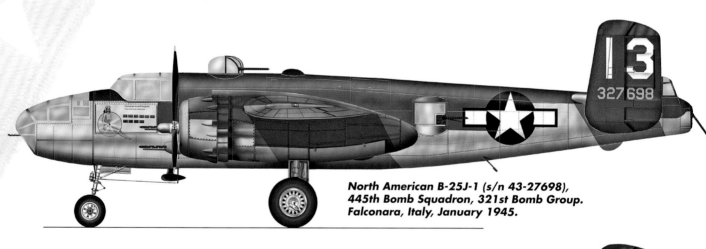

North American B-25J-1 (s/n 43-27698), 445th Bomb Squadron, 321st Bomb Group. Falconara, Italy, January 1945.

North American B-25J-1 (s/n 43-27751) "MMR", 446th Bomb Squadron, 321st Bomb Group. Solenzara, Corsica, beginning of 1945.

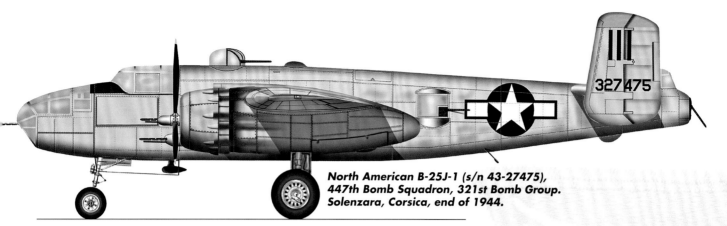

North American B-25J-1 (s/n 43-27475),
447th Bomb Squadron, 321st Bomb Group.
Solenzara, Corsica, end of 1944.

340TH BOMBARDMENT GROUP (MEDIUM)

This group, formed on the 10 August 1942, was activated ten days later on Columbia Air Force Base, South Carolina. Before joining the 9th Air Force and its first base situated at El Kabrit, Egypt on 30 March 1943, It crossed the Atlantic by the southern route with its B-25s.

Its first mission from Sfax, Tunisia took place on 19 April 1943. During its time in the 9th Air Force, the group carried out ground support missions and received a Distinguished Unit Citation for the constant effort it made during the period from April to August 1943.

On 22 August 1943, the 340th BG (M) was transferred to the 12th Air Force in which it carried out interdiction and ground support missions from bases located at Corniso and Catania, Sicily from August to October 1943, then at San Pancrazio and Foggia, Italy from October 1943 to January 1944.

After 2 January 1944 it was based at Pompei and while there, half the group's aircraft were destroyed when Vesuvius erupted on 22 March 1944 and were covered with a deluge of ash and lumps of earth. The 340th had to move to Paestum, Italy at once.

The group moved to Alesani, Corsica on 18 April 1944 then returned to Italy on the 27th to settle on the base at Rimini where it remained till the end of the war.

It was awarded a second DUC for sinking the battle cruiser Taranto in the port of la Spezia, Italy on 22 September 1944, thus preventing the Germans from scuttling this large warship and blocking the entrance to this important port.

It was at Columbia, South Carolina, that the group was disbanded on 7 November 1945

The 340th Bombardment Group (M) was made up of four squadrons:

- **486th Bomb Squadron (M)**: tactical code "6" followed by a individual letter for each plane.

No distinctive colour.

- **487th Bomb Squadron (M)**: tactical code "7" followed by a individual letter for each plane.

No distinctive colour.

- **488th Bomb Squadron (M)**: tactical code "8" followed by a individual letter for each plane.

No distinctive colour.

- **489th Bomb Squadron (M)**: tactical code "9" followed by a individual letter for each plane.

No distinctive colour.

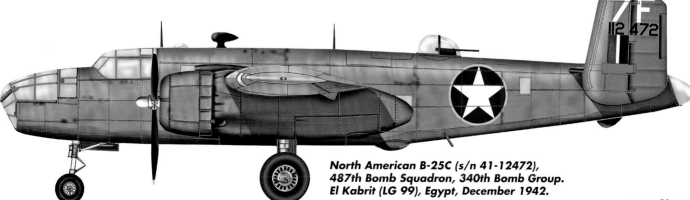

North American B-25C (s/n 41-12472),
487th Bomb Squadron, 340th Bomb Group.
El Kabrit (LG 99), Egypt, December 1942.

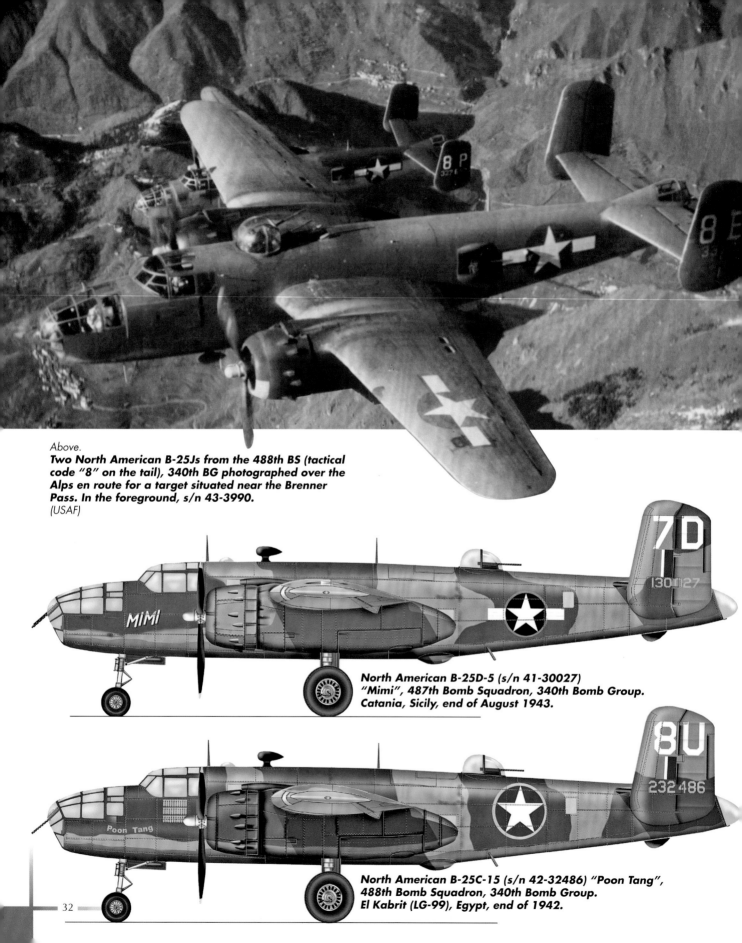

Above.
Two North American B-25Js from the 488th BS (tactical code "8" on the tail), 340th BG photographed over the Alps en route for a target situated near the Brenner Pass. In the foreground, s/n 43-3990.
(USAF)

North American B-25D-5 (s/n 41-30027) "Mimi", 487th Bomb Squadron, 340th Bomb Group. Catania, Sicily, end of August 1943.

North American B-25C-15 (s/n 42-32486) "Poon Tang", 488th Bomb Squadron, 340th Bomb Group. El Kabrit (LG-99), Egypt, end of 1942.

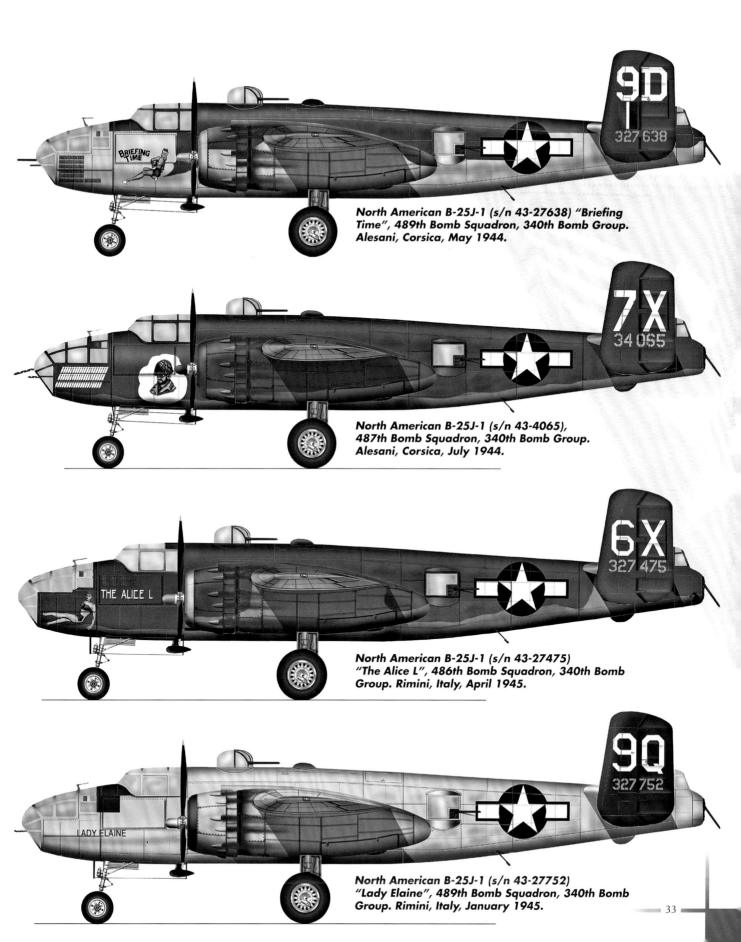

North American B-25J-1 (s/n 43-27638) "Briefing Time", 489th Bomb Squadron, 340th Bomb Group. Alesani, Corsica, May 1944.

North American B-25J-1 (s/n 43-4065), 487th Bomb Squadron, 340th Bomb Group. Alesani, Corsica, July 1944.

North American B-25J-1 (s/n 43-27475) "The Alice L", 486th Bomb Squadron, 340th Bomb Group. Rimini, Italy, April 1945.

North American B-25J-1 (s/n 43-27752) "Lady Elaine", 489th Bomb Squadron, 340th Bomb Group. Rimini, Italy, January 1945.

68TH OBSERVATION GROUP

Above. **Four F-6Cs from the 111th TRS with their engines ticking over. This was the photo reconnaissance version of the famous P-51B Mustang.** *(USAF)*

most of the squadrons were deployed to carry out various operations on the Mediterranean front.

Operating from bases at Bertaux, Algeria and Massicault, Tunisia until November 1943, the group patrolled along the Mediterranean, attacking lorries, armour, gun positions and supply depots to support the ground troops. Another of its roles was to train fighter pilots as well as replacement crews. It also carried out reconnaissance and photographic missions over Tunisia, Sicily and Italy to supply information the artillery needed. The 68th OG used different types of planes: P-38s, P-39s, P-40s, P-51s, A-20s, B-17s and B-24s.

The group then moved to Manduria in Italy and was transferred to the 15th Air Force in November 1943. Reassigned to the airfield at Blida in Algeria, it was disbanded on 15 June 1944.

The 68th Observation Group was made up of four squadrons:

-16th Reconnaissance Squadron (no tactical code and no distinctive colour).

- 111th Tactical Reconnaissance Squadron (no tactical code and no distinctive colour).

- 122nd Observation Squadron (no tactical code, no distinctive colour and no insignia).

- 154th WEA Squadron (Weather Reconnaissance Squadron) (no tactical code and no distinctive colour).

This group was formed with the name of the 68th Observation Group on 21 August 1941 then activated at Brownwood, Texas on the following 1 September. At first it carried out patrols over the Gulf of Mexico and along the Mexican border after the Japanese attack on Pearl Harbor.

The group started to train in February 1942 so it could be transferred to the Mediterranean theatre of operations where it was assigned to the 12th Air Force and based at Oujda, Morocco.

Renamed the 68th Reconnaissance Group in May 1943, then 68th Tactical Reconnaissance Group in November 1943 it was sent into the front line and

Douglas A-20B Havoc, 111th TRS, 68th TRG. Tunisia, 1943.

North American P-51A Mustang (s/n 41-37365), 111th TRS, 68th TRG. Berteaux, Algeria, end of 1943.

*North American P-51A Mustang (s/n 41-37322)
"Mah Sweet/Eva Lee", 154th Observation Squadron,
68th Observation Group. Algeria, April 1943*

3RD PHOTO GROUP (RCN)

This group was made up on 9 June 1942 and activated at Colorado Springs, Colorado, eleven days later. It was renamed the 3rd Photographic and Mapping Group in May 1943, then 3rd Photographic Group (Reconnaissance) in November 1943. It left for the Mediterranean front by the North Atlantic route and transited by Steeple Morden, Great Britain before reaching Algeria in November 1942 and being assigned to the 12th Air Force. Using Lockheed F-4s and F-5s Lightnings, it carried out photographic reconnaissance missions during the operations in Tunisia, Pantelleria, Sardinia and Sicily. At the beginning of 1944, based at Pomigliano, Italy, it covered the landing zones at Anzio and continued to recce for the 5th Army while it moved up Italy. It then moved to Corsica to cover the landings in Provence in August 1944.

The 3rd was awarded the Distinguished Unit Citation for a mission carried out on 28August 1944 which enabled it to supply photographic information which was vital for the Allied ground troops to progress rapidly.

The group ended the war in Pomigliano, Italy, in May 1945. The 3rd Photo-graphic Group comprised the following squadrons.

- **5th RCN Squadron**: (no tactical code and no distinctive colour).

- **12th RCN Squadron**: (no tactical code, no distinctive colour and no insignia).

- **15th RCN Squadron**: (no tactical code and no distinctive colour).

- **23rd RCN Squadron**: (no tactical code and no distinctive colour).

Lockheed F-5A, 3rd Photo Group. Italy, 1944.

Lockheed F-4A, 3rd Photo Group, beginning of 1943.

LES GROUPES DE CHASSE DE LA 12TH AF

1ST FIGHTER GROUP

The 1st Fighter Group, which had been created in 1918, was reformed in 1924 as the 1st Pursuit Group. It was then renamed the 1st Pursuit Group (Interceptor) in December 1939, then the 1st Pursuit Group (Fighter) in March 1941 and finally the 1st Fighter Group in May 1942.

After the Japanese attack on Pearl Harbor the group, equipped at the time with P-38s and P-43s, moved to March Field, California to carry out surveillance patrols along the United States West Coast. In June-July 1942, it was assigned to the 8th Air Force based in Great Britain and went into action at the end of August 1942, carrying out missions over France before being assigned to the 12th Air Force operating in the Mediterranean theatre of operations.

The ground crews landed at Arzew, Algeria on 8 November 1942 at the same time as the assault troops. The crews arrived with their P-38s on 13 November and settled at Tafaraoui, Algeria where they were immediately operational, attacking enemy shipping and carrying out bomber escort missions as well as ground attack missions during the Tunisian Campaign. In June 1943, the group was based at Mateur, Tunisia taking part

Four pilots from the 27th FS, 1st FG proudly show off the tail of a German machine as a war trophy in front of Lockheed P-38G s/n 43-2308 nicknamed "Shoot, You're Faded". From left to right: Second Lieutenant John A. MacKay, the Lightning's usual pilot and officially credited with six kills, 2nd Lt Samuel F. Sweet (4 kills), 2nd Lt Warren A. Holden (2 kills) and 1st Lt Frank J. McIntosh (3 kills). (USAF)

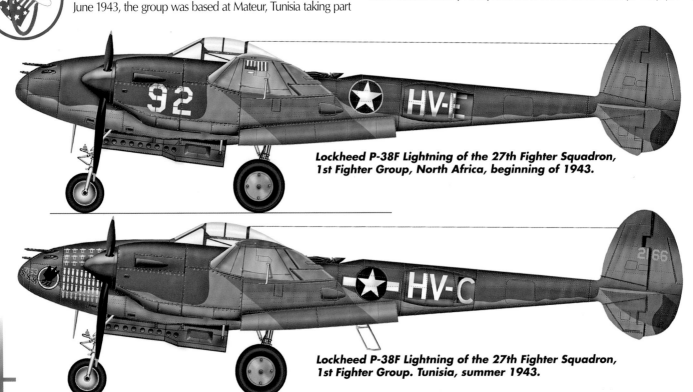

Lockheed P-38F Lightning of the 27th Fighter Squadron, 1st Fighter Group, North Africa, beginning of 1943.

Lockheed P-38F Lightning of the 27th Fighter Squadron, 1st Fighter Group. Tunisia, summer 1943.

fields on 25 August 1943, destroying a large number of planes which were a serious threat to the troops landing at Salerno. It was awarded a second DUC for its action on 30 August 1943 escorting bombers over Italy, and driving off enemy fighters, thereby enabling the bombers to inflict serious damage on the marshalling yards at Aversa.

The 1st fighter Group continued its operations in the 12th Air Force until November 1943 from its base at Cagliari, Sardinia before being assigned to the 15th Air Force.

The 1st Fighter Group comprised three squadrons:

- **27th Fighter Squadron**: tactical code "HV", red distinctive colour.

- **71st Fighter Squadron**: tactical code "LM", white distinctive colour.

- **94th Fighter Squadron**: tactical code "UN", yellow distinctive colour.

in the attacks on the island of Pantelleria, escorting bombers over targets in Sicily and carrying out air support operations for the ground troops.

It was while it was carrying out missions over Italy that the 1st Fighter Group was awarded a Distinguished Unit Citation for attacking Italian air-

On the airfield at Lesina, Italy a mechanic from the 94th FS poses proudly in the car he has made using a Lightning drop tank... In the background is P-38L s/n 44-25734 "Betts II", 71st Fighter Squadron, which was shot down on 15 April 1945 while strafing railway lines in the Munich region. (USAF)

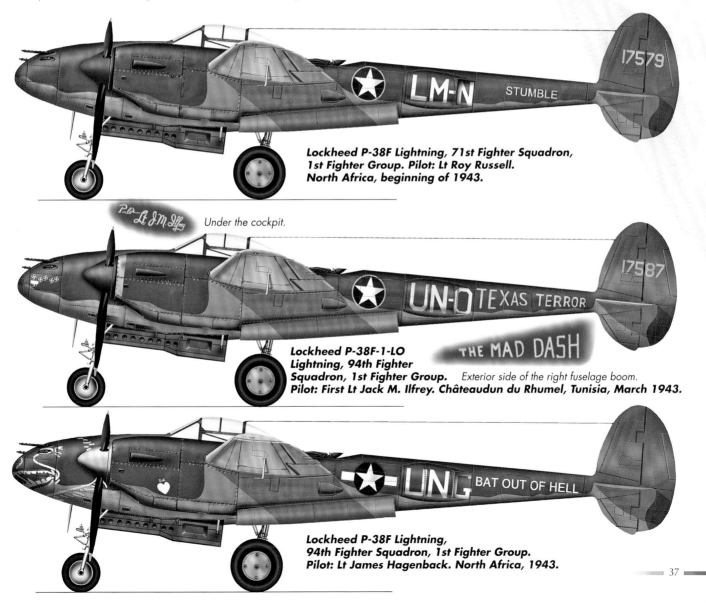

Lockheed P-38F Lightning, 71st Fighter Squadron, 1st Fighter Group. Pilot: Lt Roy Russell. North Africa, beginning of 1943.

Under the cockpit.

Lockheed P-38F-1-LO Lightning, 94th Fighter Squadron, 1st Fighter Group. Pilot: First Lt Jack M. Ilfrey. Châteaudun du Rhumel, Tunisia, March 1943.

Exterior side of the right fuselage boom.

Lockheed P-38F Lightning, 94th Fighter Squadron, 1st Fighter Group. Pilot: Lt James Hagenback. North Africa, 1943.

14TH FIGHTER GROUP

The 14th Pursuit Group was activated on 15 January 1941 at Hamilton Field, California and started training in June 1941 at March Field, California with Curtiss P-40s, P-43 Lancers, and P-38Ds and Es. Equipped later with P-38s it carried out surveillance patrols along the United States West Coast after the Japanese attacked Pearl Harbor.

In May 1942, the 14th Pursuit Group was renamed the 14th Fighter Group just before being sent to Great Britain which the ground crews reached in August 1942. The P-38s taking off from Bradly Field Connecticut reached England by the North Atlantic route on 1 July 1942. The group, assigned to the 8th Air Force, settled on the RAF base at Atcham.

On 14 September 1942 it was reassigned to the 12th Air Force but continued operating under the command of the 8th Air Force until mid-October, carrying out sweeps over France.

The ground crews of the 14th Fighter Group embarked for Algeria and reached Oran on 10 November 1942. The P-38s moved rapidly to the airfield at Tafaraoui (14 November) taking part in operations immediately,

carrying out escort, ground attack and recce missions from various bases located in Algeria. In January, because the personnel had been assigned to other fighter groups, the 14th Fighter Group stopped operating for a short while, but resumed fighting in May 1943 after being given newer Lightning versions (P-38F and G).

In June 1943, the group moved to El Bathan, Tunisia. The 12th Air force prepared the landings in Sicily on 10 July 1943 for Operation Husky, intensifying its attacks against Sicily and the islands of Pantelleria and Lampedusa. Lieutenant H.T. Hanna of the 14th Fighter Group became an ace in a single day, destroying five Junker Ju 87s on 9 October 1943.

In November 1943 the 14th Fighter Group was reassigned to the 15th Air Force while still based in Tunisia.

The 14th Fighter Group was made up of three squadrons:
- **37th Fighter Squadron**: no tactical code and red distinctive colour.
- **48th Fighter Squadron**: tactical code "ES" and white distinctive colour.
- **49th Fighter Squadron**: tactical code "QU" and blue distinctive colour.

Above. **Lieutenant Richard A. Campbell, 37th FS, 14th FG posing in front of his P-38 baptised "Earthquake/McGoon". Five kills, including an Italian one, have been painted at the front.** *(USAF)*

Lockheed P-38-G-15-LO "Kay" of the 37th Fighter Squadron, 14th Fighter Group. Pilot: Lt James Hollingsworth. North Africa, June 1943.

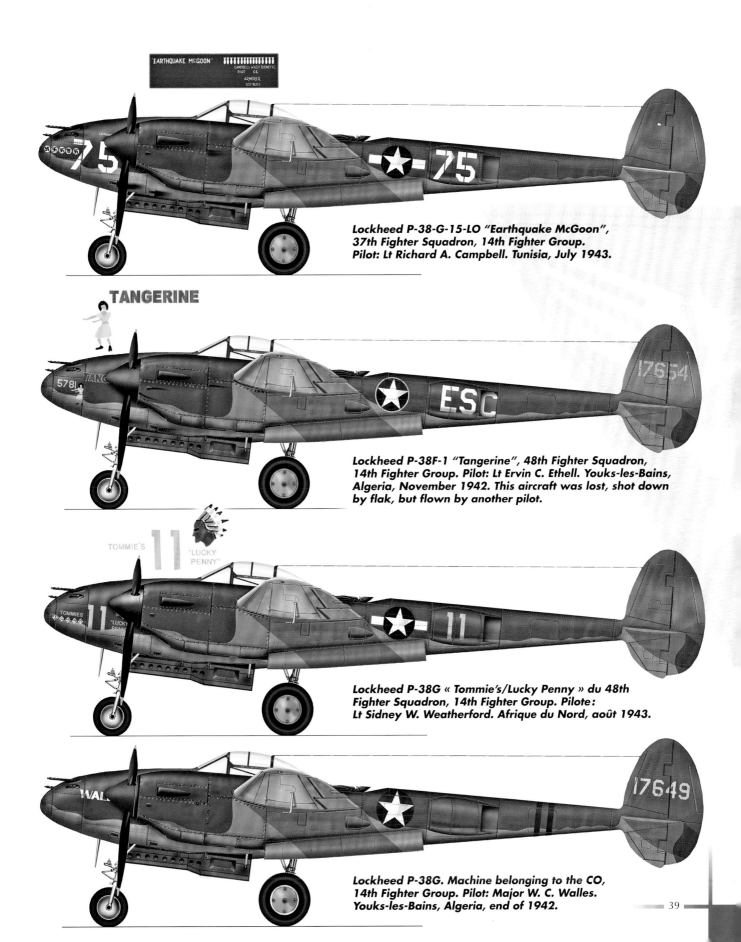

"EARTHQUAKE McGOON"

Lockheed P-38-G-15-LO "Earthquake McGoon",
37th Fighter Squadron, 14th Fighter Group.
Pilot: Lt Richard A. Campbell. Tunisia, July 1943.

TANGERINE

Lockheed P-38F-1 "Tangerine", 48th Fighter Squadron,
14th Fighter Group. Pilot: Lt Ervin C. Ethell. Youks-les-Bains,
Algeria, November 1942. This aircraft was lost, shot down
by flak, but flown by another pilot.

TOMMIE'S 11 "LUCKY PENNY"

Lockheed P-38G « Tommie's/Lucky Penny » du 48th
Fighter Squadron, 14th Fighter Group. Pilote:
Lt Sidney W. Weatherford. Afrique du Nord, août 1943.

Lockheed P-38G. Machine belonging to the CO,
14th Fighter Group. Pilot: Major W. C. Walles.
Youks-les-Bains, Algeria, end of 1942.

A North American A-36A Apache of the 27th Fighter Group, Korba, Tunisia in 1943 being maintained under particularly delicate conditions. The plane has two swastikas indicating kills on the front of the fuselage, near the machine gun port. (USAF)

27TH FIGHTER GROUP

This group, activated on 1 February 1941 at Barksdale Field, Louisiana under the name of the 27th Bombardment Group (Light) should originally have been based in the Philippines, but after Pearl Harbor it was redirected to Australia. Sent stateside in May 1942 to be re-formed and issued with Douglas A-20 attack bombers, it trained until it was sent to Algeria in November of the same year.

There it joined the 12th Air Force after converting to the North American A-36 Apache in June 1943; in the following August it was renamed the 27th Fighter-Bomber Group. From February to June 1944 the group flew P-40s and in May of the same year, it was renamed the 27th Fighter Group.

In June 1944, the 27th FG squadrons were again converted, this time to Republic P-47s while based at Ciampino, Italy.

With the Allies landing in Provence (Operation Dragon) on 15 August 1944, the group, based at Serragia, Corsica gave air cover to the US VII Army while it made its way up the Rhone Valley.

On 4 September 1944, the group carried out thirteen missions and 58 sorties from its departure base

at Santa Maria, Italy, situated more than 300 km from the combat zones. Because of the distance, the group had to have drop tanks, but there were so few of them at the time that the pilots were ordered not to drop them when they were empty.

The low altitude air support operations resulted in a lot of damage and losses for the P-47s, particularly from the German flak. Nonetheless the group destroyed 107 vehicles, 30 mobile cannon, twelve locomotives and slowed down eleven trains, of which some were transporting heavy artillery, all of which obviously seriously hampered the Germans as they were falling back. Thanks to these operations the 27th Fighter Group was awarded its fifth DUC.

In October 1944, the 27th Fighter Group moved to Tarquinia, Italy to cut the German lines of communication in Northern Italy. Later, it took part in the Allied advance from the south of France into Germany during the final phase of the war. In February 1945, the group operated from Saint-Dizier, France as part of the 1st Tactical Air Force and finished the war in Germany.

The 27th Fighter Group was made up of three squadrons:
- **522nd Fighter Squadron**: tactical code B, red distinctive colour rouge.
- **523rd Fighter Squadron**: tactical code C, blue distinctive colour.
- **524th Fighter Squadron**: tactical code A, yellow distinctive colour.

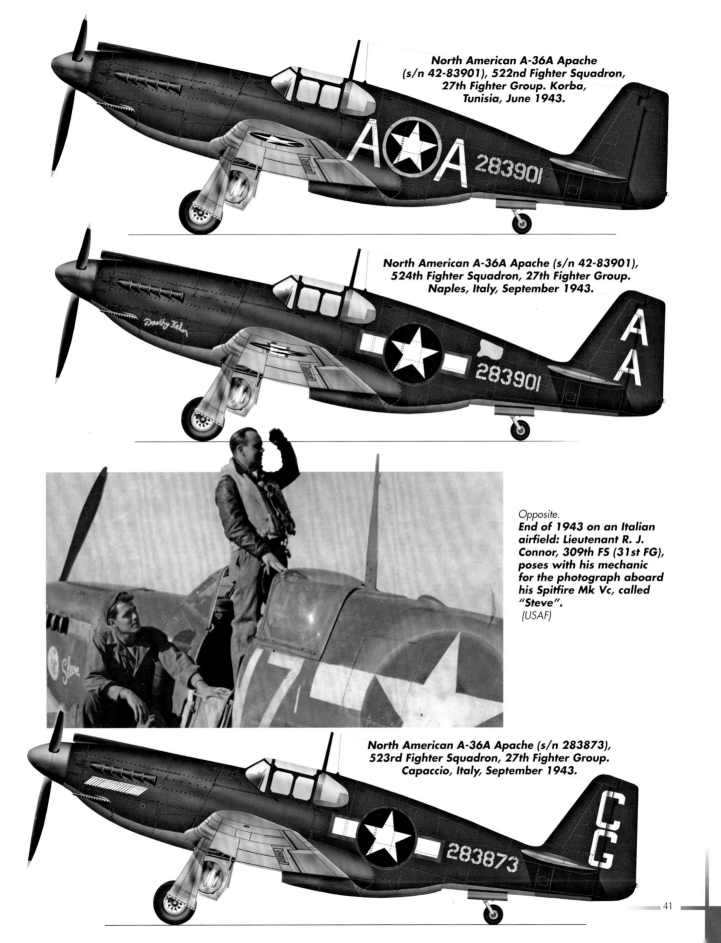

North American A-36A Apache
(s/n 42-83901), 522nd Fighter Squadron,
27th Fighter Group. Korba,
Tunisia, June 1943.

North American A-36A Apache (s/n 42-83901),
524th Fighter Squadron, 27th Fighter Group.
Naples, Italy, September 1943.

Opposite.
**End of 1943 on an Italian
airfield: Lieutenant R. J.
Connor, 309th FS (31st FG),
poses with his mechanic
for the photograph aboard
his Spitfire Mk Vc, called
"Steve".**
(USAF)

North American A-36A Apache (s/n 283873),
523rd Fighter Squadron, 27th Fighter Group.
Capaccio, Italy, September 1943.

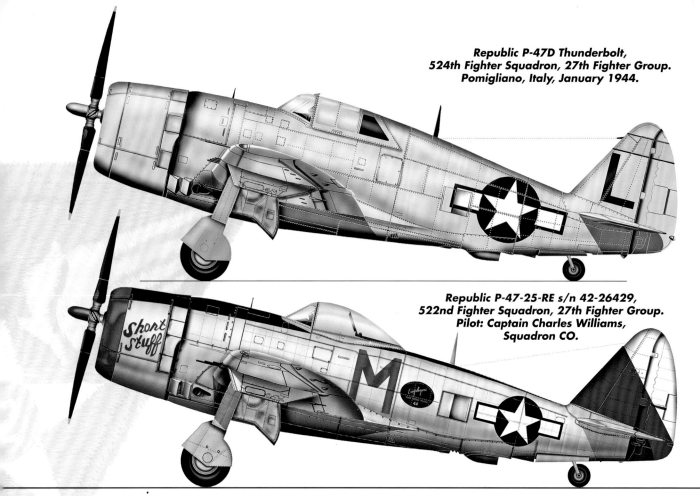

*Republic P-47D Thunderbolt,
524th Fighter Squadron, 27th Fighter Group.
Pomigliano, Italy, January 1944.*

*Republic P-47-25-RE s/n 42-26429,
522nd Fighter Squadron, 27th Fighter Group.
Pilot: Captain Charles Williams,
Squadron CO.*

31ST FIGHTER GROUP

This group was created on 22 December 1939 and called the 31st Pursuit Group (Interceptor). Activated on 1 February 1940, it trained on P-39s. In May 1942, it was renamed the 31st Fighter Group, assigned to the 8th Air Force based in Great Britain and equipped with Spitfires. In August 1942 it took part in its first combat missions, including a raid on Dieppe, France on 19 August, which was followed by a variety of other missions until October.

In order to support the landings in North Africa, the 31st FG was assigned to the 12th Air Force and sent to Tafaraoui on 8 November 1942 after transiting by Gibraltar with its Spitfires and with the ground crews reaching Arzew, Algeria on the same day. The group attacked troop concentrations, artillery positions and transport vehicles during the three days that the Algerian and Moroccan campaigns lasted.

*Spitfire Mk IX, 307th FS, 31st FG on an Italian base.
The planes still bear the original British markings,
in particular their serial number on the rear
of the fuselage. (USAF)*

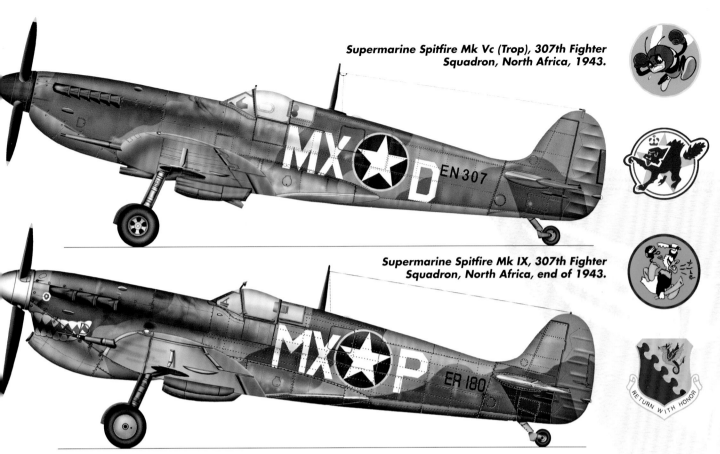

Supermarine Spitfire Mk Vc (Trop), 307th Fighter Squadron, North Africa, 1943.

Supermarine Spitfire Mk IX, 307th Fighter Squadron, North Africa, end of 1943.

While it was based at Youks-les Bains, Algeria, it took part in defeating the Axis forces in Tunisia by supporting ground troops and by escorting bombers. In May 1943, at the end of the campaign, it was based at Korba, Tunisia.

During May and June 1943, based on Gozo, Malta, it escorted bombers during raids against the island of Pantelleria and gave covering support for convoys sailing in the Mediterranean. It then supported the landings in Sicily in July 1943 and took part conquering the island. On 13 July, the 31st FG settled at Ponto Olivo, Sicily.

In September 1943, the group supported the landings at Salerno, Italy and in January 1944, those at Anzio in Italy,

carrying out support missions for the ground forces in Italy and escorting bombers.

It was on the base at San Severo, Italy in April 1944 that the 31st Fighter Group was transferred to the 15th Air Force and converted at the same time to P-51 Mustangs.

The 31st Fighter Group was made up of three squadrons:
- **307th Fighter Squadron**: tactical code "MX", no distinctive colour.
- **308th Fighter Squadron**: tactical code "HL", no distinctive colour
- **309th Fighter Squadron**: tactical code "WZ", no distinctive colour.

Supermarine Spitfire Mk Vb (JK226/HL°AA), 308th Fighter Squadron, Tafaraoui, Algeria, end of 1942.

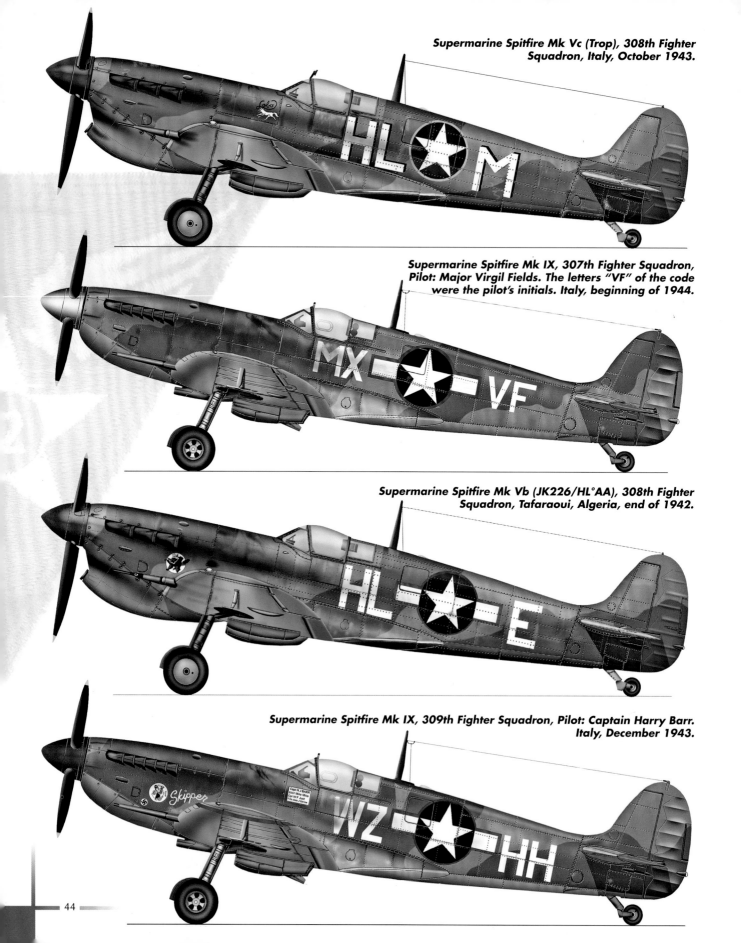

Supermarine Spitfire Mk Vc (Trop), 308th Fighter Squadron, Italy, October 1943.

Supermarine Spitfire Mk IX, 307th Fighter Squadron, Pilot: Major Virgil Fields. The letters "VF" of the code were the pilot's initials. Italy, beginning of 1944.

Supermarine Spitfire Mk Vb (JK226/HL°AA), 308th Fighter Squadron, Tafaraoui, Algeria, end of 1942.

Supermarine Spitfire Mk IX, 309th Fighter Squadron, Pilot: Captain Harry Barr. Italy, December 1943.

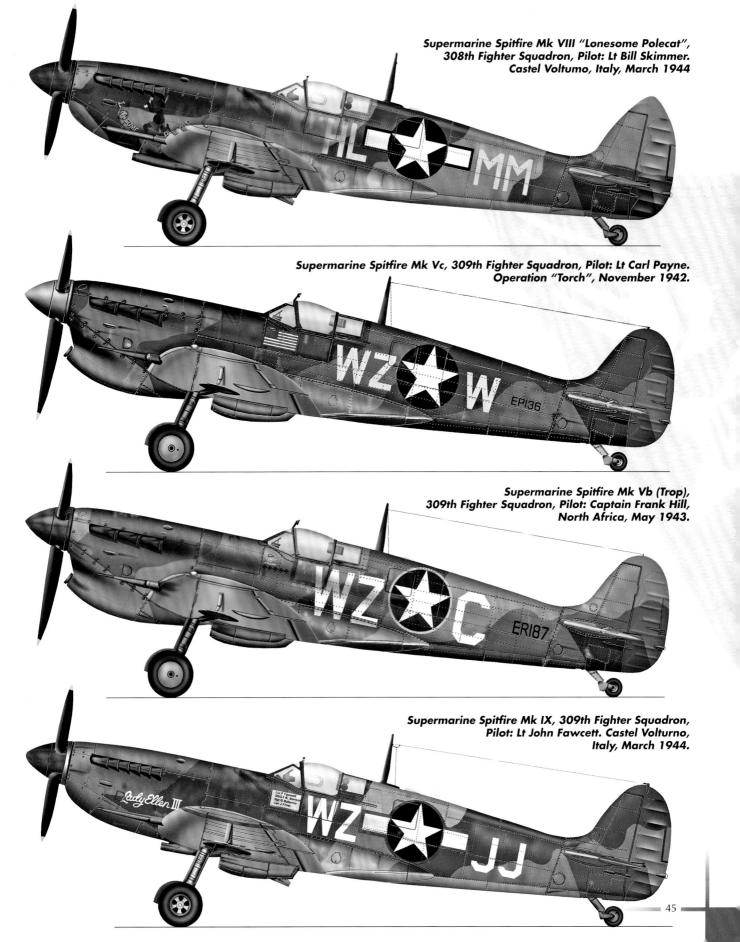

Supermarine Spitfire Mk VIII "Lonesome Polecat",
308th Fighter Squadron, Pilot: Lt Bill Skimmer.
Castel Voltumo, Italy, March 1944

Supermarine Spitfire Mk Vc, 309th Fighter Squadron, Pilot: Lt Carl Payne.
Operation "Torch", November 1942.

Supermarine Spitfire Mk Vb (Trop),
309th Fighter Squadron, Pilot: Captain Frank Hill,
North Africa, May 1943.

Supermarine Spitfire Mk IX, 309th Fighter Squadron,
Pilot: Lt John Fawcett. Castel Volturno,
Italy, March 1944.

33RD FIGHTER GROUP

The 33rd Pursuit Group was made up on 20 November 1940 and activated on 15 January 1941, starting its training on P-39s then changing quickly to P-40s. After the Japanese attack on Pearl Harbor, it was assigned to defending of the East Coat of the United States.

In May 1942 it was renamed the 33rd Fighter Group and assigned to the 12th Air Force. Embarking aboard the carrier, *USS Ranger*, its P-40s took off just off the Moroccan coast to reach the airfield at Port Lyautey, Morocco, on 10 November 1942.

It left Morocco at the end of December 1942 to move to Telergma, Algeria in order to take part in the whole of the North African Campaign where it carried out ground attack and bombing missions against troop concentrations, port installations, fuel depots as well as bridges, roads and railway lines.

The group was awarded a Distinguished Unit Citation while set up at Thelepte, Tunisia for its action on 15 January 1943 when during an enemy attack it dispersed the escorting fighters and shot down a lot of

A P-40F from the 58th FS (33rd FG) taking off from the carrier, USS Ranger, during Operation "Torch" on 10 November 1942. The machines bore the star spangled banner on the fuselage and under the port wing as well as their usual national roundels. (USAF)

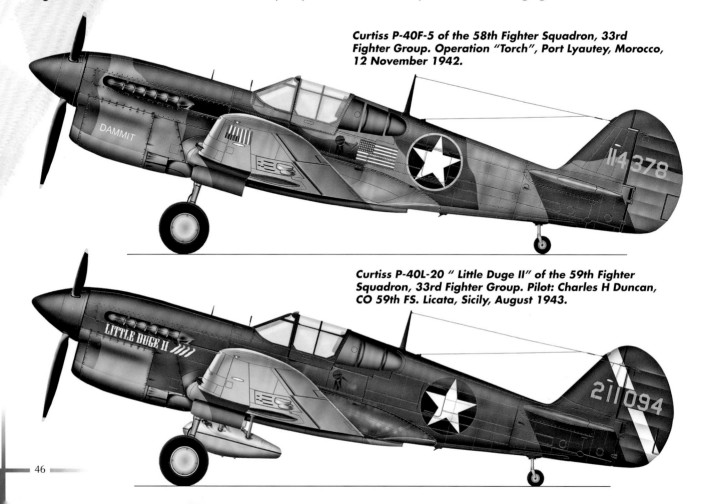

Curtiss P-40F-5 of the 58th Fighter Squadron, 33rd Fighter Group. Operation "Torch", Port Lyautey, Morocco, 12 November 1942.

DAMMIT

114378

Curtiss P-40L-20 " Little Duge II" of the 59th Fighter Squadron, 33rd Fighter Group. Pilot: Charles H Duncan, CO 59th FS. Licata, Sicily, August 1943.

LITTLE DUGE II

211094

the bombers. It took part in reducing the island of Pantelleria, carrying out patrols until the enemy garrison surrendered; it also took part in the landings in Sicily and in conquering the island before settling at Licata, Sicily in July 1943. Later, the 33rd FG supported the landings at Salerno, Italy, the Allied operations in the south of the country and the Anzio bridgehead. In September it settled at Paestum, near Naples and in the end was assigned to the 10th Air force fighting in India in February 1944.

The 33rd Fighter Group was made up of:

- **58th Fighter Squadron**: no tactical code but a slanting red stripe on the tail fin.
- **59th Fighter Squadron**: no tactical code but a slanting white stripe on the tail fin.
- **60th Fighter Squadron**: no tactical code but a slanting yellow stripe on the tail fin.

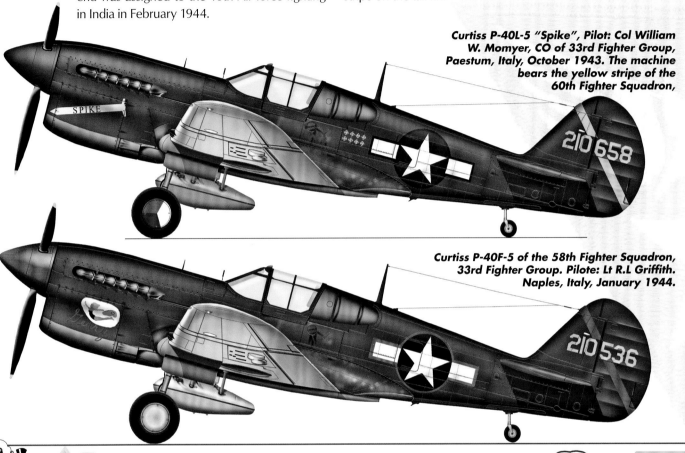

Curtiss P-40L-5 "Spike", Pilot: Col William W. Momyer, CO of 33rd Fighter Group, Paestum, Italy, October 1943. The machine bears the yellow stripe of the 60th Fighter Squadron,

Curtiss P-40F-5 of the 58th Fighter Squadron, 33rd Fighter Group. Pilote: Lt R.L Griffith. Naples, Italy, January 1944.

52ND FIGHTER GROUP

It was on 15 January 1941 that the 52nd Pursuit Group (Interceptor) was activated. It was renamed 52nd Fighter Group in May 1942, its pilots training on P-39s and P-40s and taking part in combat exercises. It was sent to Great Britain without planes and attached to the 8th Air Force in July 1942 when it received its Spitfires with which it carried out missions over France in August and September of the same year.

In order to take part in the North African Campaign, after transiting by Gibraltar, the group settled at Tafaraoui, Algeria with its fighters. Assigned to the 12th Air Force in Novem-

ber 1942, it then took part in the Mediterranean theatre combat operations.

During the North African Campaign, it was based in Algeria and Tunisia, its last airfield being at la Sebala, Tunisia in May 1943. The 52nd FG was given the task of carrying out patrols, escort, ground attack and reconnaissance missions all contributing to defeating the Axis forces in Tunisia. In July 1943, it settled on the airfield of Bocca di Falco, Sicily and ended the year at Calvi, Corsica. It then took part in the conquest of Sicily and attacked railway lines, main roads, bridges, coasters and other targets, and backing up the Allied operations in Italy.

It converted to P-51s in April and May 1944 and was the transferred to the 15th Air Force.

The 52nd Fighter Squadron comprised three squadrons:
- **2nd Fighter Squadron**, tactical code "QP", no distinctive colour.
- **4th Fighter Squadron**, tactical code "WD", no distinctive colour.
- **5th Fighter Squadron**, tactical code "VF", no distinctive colour.

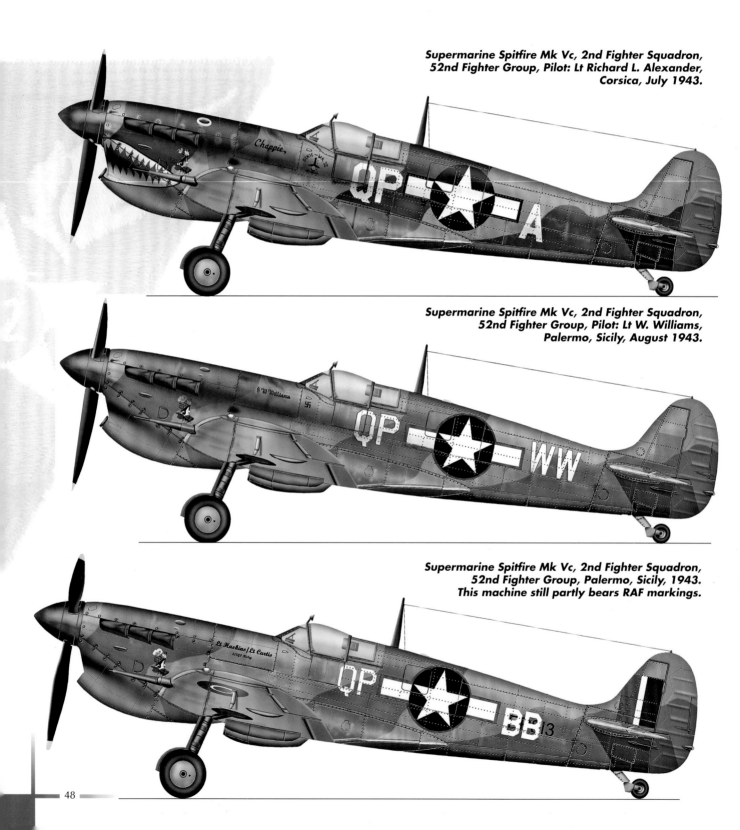

Supermarine Spitfire Mk Vc, 2nd Fighter Squadron, 52nd Fighter Group, Pilot: Lt Richard L. Alexander, Corsica, July 1943.

Supermarine Spitfire Mk Vc, 2nd Fighter Squadron, 52nd Fighter Group, Pilot: Lt W. Williams, Palermo, Sicily, August 1943.

Supermarine Spitfire Mk Vc, 2nd Fighter Squadron, 52nd Fighter Group, Palermo, Sicily, 1943. This machine still partly bears RAF markings.

Supermarine Spitfire Mk IX, 2nd Fighter Squadron, 52nd Fighter Group, Pilot: Lt F. Ohr, Palermo, Sicily, 1943

57TH FIGHTER GROUP

The 57th Pursuit Group was constituted on 20 November 1940. After settling with its ground crews on the base at Mitchell Park, New York on 15 January 1941, it started its training on Curtiss P-40s. In May 1942, it was renamed the 57th Fighter Group and sent to Egypt, assigned to the Desert Air Force in July 1942. It was there that it joined the 9th Air Force between July and November 1942 after training with the RAF. It became operational on P-40s in October of the same year and started operations in the Libyan Desert. It ended this campaign at Zuara in February 1943 then took part in the Tunisian Campaign.

The 66th Squadron, belonging to the 57th FG and based at Al Djem, Tunisia was nicknamed the "X-terminators" by a German radio program called "Axis Sally" following the carnage on Palm Sunday, 18 April 1943, when fifty-nine Junkers Ju 52 transport planes laden with troops and supplies together with sixteen fighter escorts en route for North Africa were

*Above. **Major Arthur G. Salisbury, Co of 57th FG from December 1942 to April 1944, photographed in a Curtiss P-40F, code "47" belonging to the 64th FS.** (USAF)*

Curtiss P-40F-10 (s/n 41-14596), 64th FS, 57th FG. Pilot: Captain A. Exon, CO of 64th FS, Scordia, Sicily, August 1943.

"SWEET STUFF"

intercepted and shot down by a group of seventy American P-40s and Spitfires. During the program, "Axis Sally" announced that the Luftwaffe would deal with this "X Squadron" which had shot down unarmed transport planes in such a cowardly manner.

The 57th Fighter Group joined the 12th Air Force in August 1943 with its P-40s and was based at Sordia, Sicily. It was at Amendola, Italy that the unit converted to P-47s in December 1943, becoming the first unit in the 12th Air Force to go over to this type of plane.

Operation "Strangle", planned to prevent German supplies from reaching the Italian front, was launched on 19 March 1944 with the aim of helping the Allied ground forces advance towards Rome. The 57th Fighter Group left Italy to settle on a new base at Alto, Corsica on 30 March from which it was to operate as a special detachment, carrying out at least 48 sorties a day.

From the 1 to 14 May 1944, the group carried out on average 80 sorties a day and on 14 April, it reached a peak of 91 sorties between 8.00

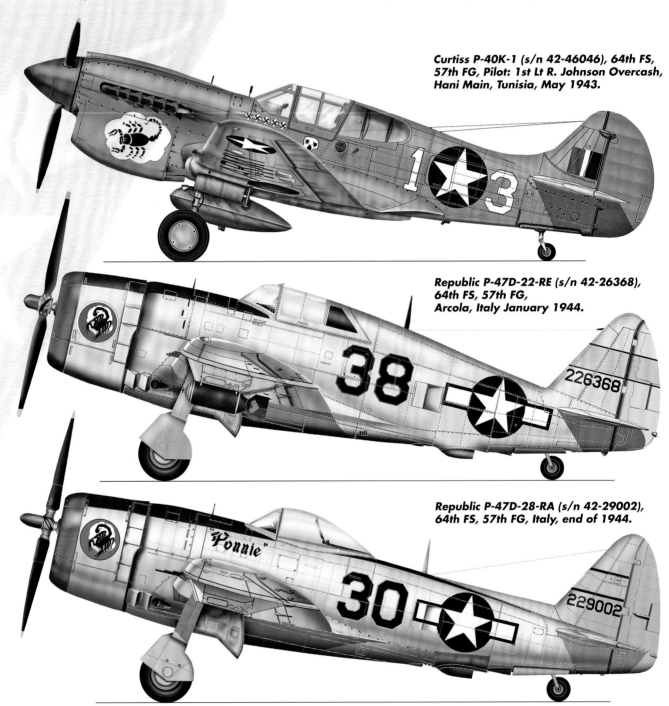

Curtiss P-40K-1 (s/n 42-46046), 64th FS, 57th FG, Pilot: 1st Lt R. Johnson Overcash, Hani Main, Tunisia, May 1943.

Republic P-47D-22-RE (s/n 42-26368), 64th FS, 57th FG, Arcola, Italy January 1944.

Republic P-47D-28-RA (s/n 42-29002), 64th FS, 57th FG, Italy, end of 1944.

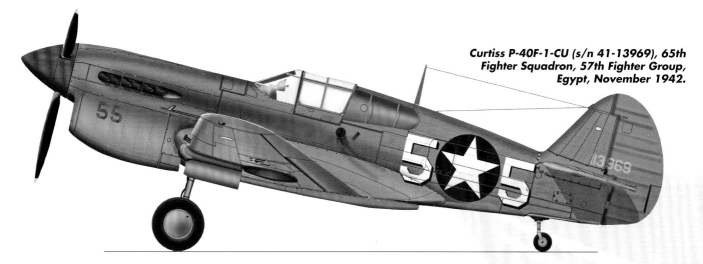

Curtiss P-40F-1-CU (s/n 41-13969), 65th Fighter Squadron, 57th Fighter Group, Egypt, November 1942.

and 16.00, carrying out six missions in the Florence-Arezzo region in Italy. The attacks and air raids carried out by the 57th FG blocked two tunnels, destroyed a railway bridge, six locomotives and 108 wagons; they also cut the railways in nine different places and destroyed a fuel dump. A dogfight took place with Me 109s and Fw 190s, a formation of twelve P-47s in the group claiming three German fighters shot down for the loss of a single Thunderbolt. Theses actions were rewarded with a DUC.

In June 1944 while still based in Corsica, the 57th Fighter Group took an active part in preparing the landings in Provence. The group then concentrated on support and interdiction missions against the Germans and their Italian allies in Northern Italy from September 1944 to May 1945.

The tactical nature of the group meant it moved several times along the Italian peninsula during 1944 and 1945. In September 1944, the group was installed at Grosseto, Italy and on 28 April 1945, it settled at Villa Franca di Verona, where it remained until the final victory.

The 57th Fighter Group was made up of three squadrons:

- **64th Fighter Squadron** ("Black Scorpions"): tactical code from 10 to 39, no distinctive colour.

- **65th Fighter Squadron** ("Fighting Cocks"): tactical code from 49 to 69, no distinctive colour.

- **66th Fighter Squadron** ("X-terminators"): tactical code from 79 to 99, no distinctive colour.

Below.
Mechanics installing rockets in the underwing "bazooka" tubes of P-47D s/n 42-76012, 65th FS whose insignia painted on the engine cowling can be seen clearly.
(USAF)

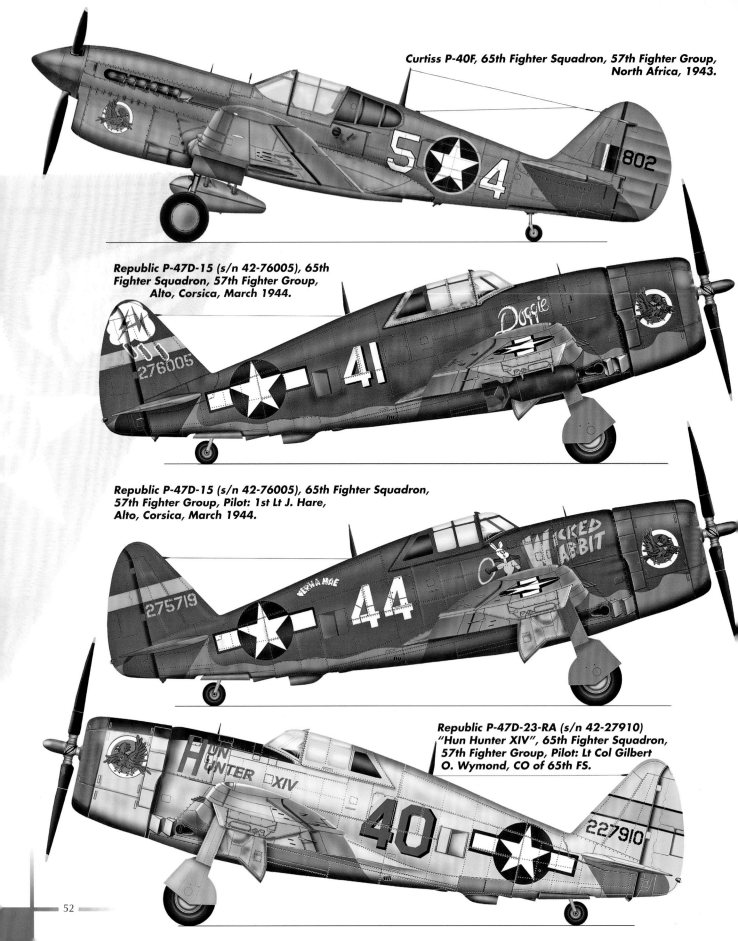

Curtiss P-40F, 65th Fighter Squadron, 57th Fighter Group, North Africa, 1943.

Republic P-47D-15 (s/n 42-76005), 65th Fighter Squadron, 57th Fighter Group, Alto, Corsica, March 1944.

Republic P-47D-15 (s/n 42-76005), 65th Fighter Squadron, 57th Fighter Group, Pilot: 1st Lt J. Hare, Alto, Corsica, March 1944.

Republic P-47D-23-RA (s/n 42-27910) "Hun Hunter XIV", 65th Fighter Squadron, 57th Fighter Group, Pilot: Lt Col Gilbert O. Wymond, CO of 65th FS.

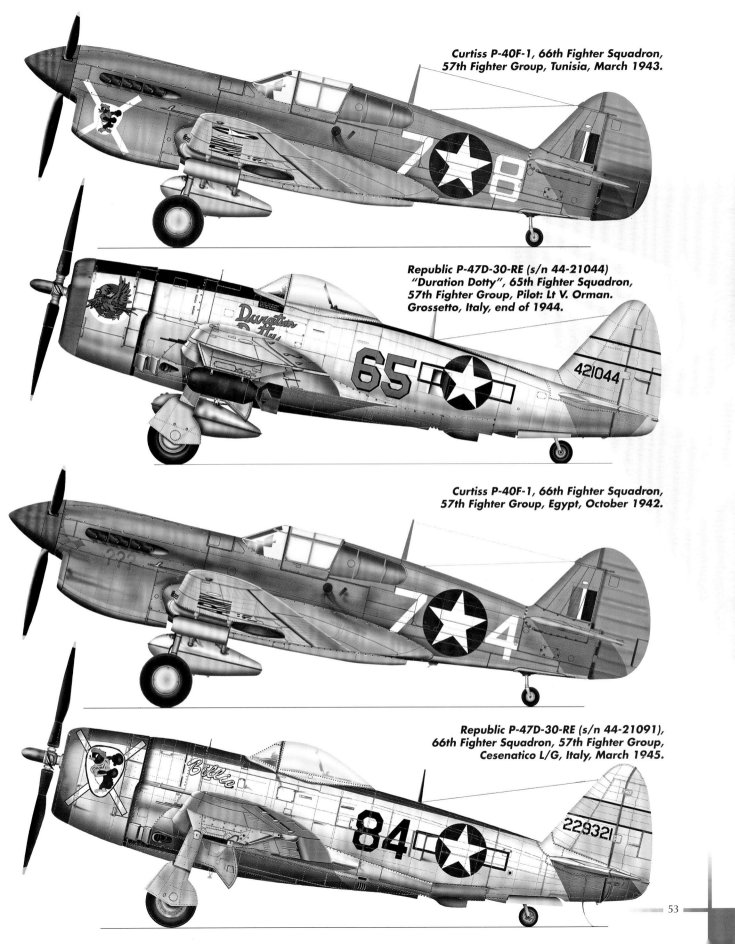

Curtiss P-40F-1, 66th Fighter Squadron,
57th Fighter Group, Tunisia, March 1943.

Republic P-47D-30-RE (s/n 44-21044)
"Duration Dotty", 65th Fighter Squadron,
57th Fighter Group, Pilot: Lt V. Orman.
Grossetto, Italy, end of 1944.

Curtiss P-40F-1, 66th Fighter Squadron,
57th Fighter Group, Egypt, October 1942.

Republic P-47D-30-RE (s/n 44-21091),
66th Fighter Squadron, 57th Fighter Group,
Cesenatico L/G, Italy, March 1945.

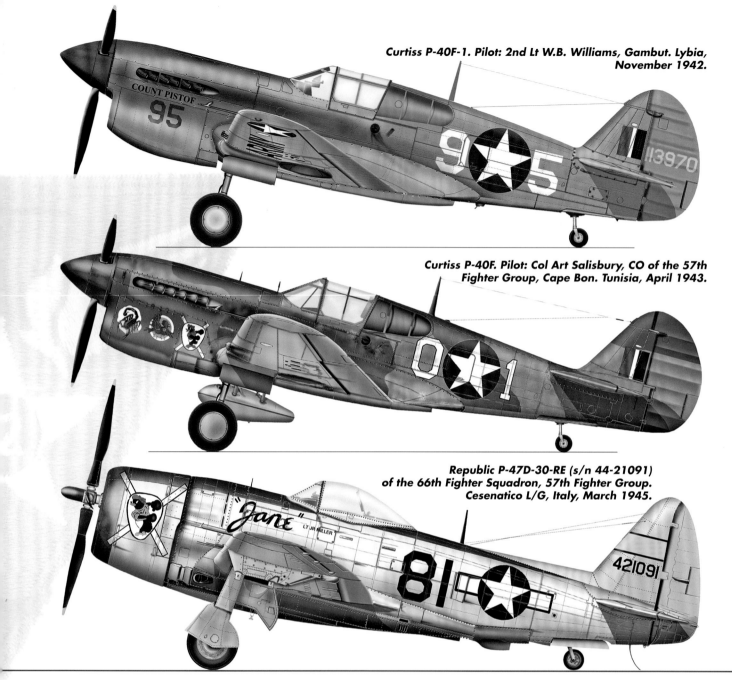

Curtiss P-40F-1. Pilot: 2nd Lt W.B. Williams, Gambut. Lybia, November 1942.

Curtiss P-40F. Pilot: Col Art Salisbury, CO of the 57th Fighter Group, Cape Bon. Tunisia, April 1943.

Republic P-47D-30-RE (s/n 44-21091) of the 66th Fighter Squadron, 57th Fighter Group. Cesenatico L/G, Italy, March 1945.

79TH FIGHTER GROUP

It was at Dale Mabry Field, near Tallahassee, Florida that the 79th Pursuit Group was created on 13 January 1942, then activated on the following 9 February and finally renamed 79th Fighter Group in May. Before joining the 9th Air Force in the Middle East, the 79th Fighter Group did its training on P-40s.

Set up in Egypt on 18 November 1942, the 79th took part in the North African Campaign in the 9th Air Force and when it left for Great Britain, it was transferred to the 12th Air Force on 22 August 1943.

On 15 March 1944, after starting to convert to P-47s, the group supported the Allied troops fighting at the Battle of Monte Cassino and obtained the first kill obtained by a P-47 against an Me-109. During April, in spite of the bad weather, the 79th Fighter Group succeeded in carrying out 168 missions. In June 1944, the group, based on the airfield at Serragia, Corsica, was entirely equipped with P-47s. It took part in supporting Operation "Dragon", the Allied landings in Provence on 15 August 1944 and then moved along the various bases in the south of France before returning to Italy.

On 3 October, the 79th Fighter Group came under the command of the Desert Air Force and settled at Lesi, Italy to support the British VIII Army. It thus became the first group of the VIII Army's front to be equipped with the three-tube underwing bazooka and it was on 19 October 1944 that the group carried out its first mission with this type of weapon. The same month, the group carried out one of its first missions over Yugoslavia to support the advance of the Russians in the Balkans, but bad weather conditions slowed operations down during the winter months. In December 1944, the group was based at Fano, Italy on the Adriatic coast and a month later, it carried out its 30 000th combat sortie.

Above. **A mechanic working on the engine of P-40 "Available Jones", 86th FS whose insignia can be seen painted on either side of the front of the fuselage.**
(USAF)

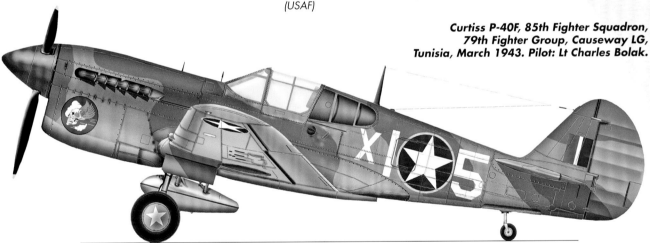

Curtiss P-40F, 85th Fighter Squadron, 79th Fighter Group, Causeway LG, Tunisia, March 1943. Pilot: Lt Charles Bolak.

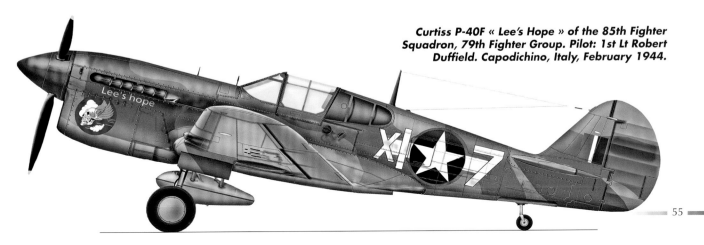

Curtiss P-40F « Lee's Hope » of the 85th Fighter Squadron, 79th Fighter Group. Pilot: 1st Lt Robert Duffield. Capodichino, Italy, February 1944.

The 79th Fighter Group's tactical missions carried on during the winter of 1944-45, until spring 1945. For 17 days in a row, the group flew more than a hundred P-47s per day and from 16 to 20 April, its daily sorties reached more than 160. Moreover the group was awarded a Distinguished Unit Citation for its activities during this period.

From 25 April to 1 May 1945 while they were stationed at Cesenatico, Italy, the group's planes carried out sweeps over Northern Italy. The war mission of 1 May 1945 turned end out to be their last. The 79th Fighter Group ended the war with 29 kills with P-47 Thunderbolts.

The 79th Fighter Group as made up of three squadrons:
- **85th Fighter Squadron** ("Flying Skulls"): tactical code from 10 to 39, no distinctive colour attributed.
- **86th Fighter Squadron** ("Comanches"): tactical code from 40 to 69, no distinctive colour attributed.
- **87th Fighter Squadron** ("Skeeters"): tactical code from code 70 to 99, no distinctive colour attributed.

Opposite. **Returning from a missions some P-40s, 79th FG, make a low altitude fly past over their airfield at Capodichino shortly before landing.**
(USAF)

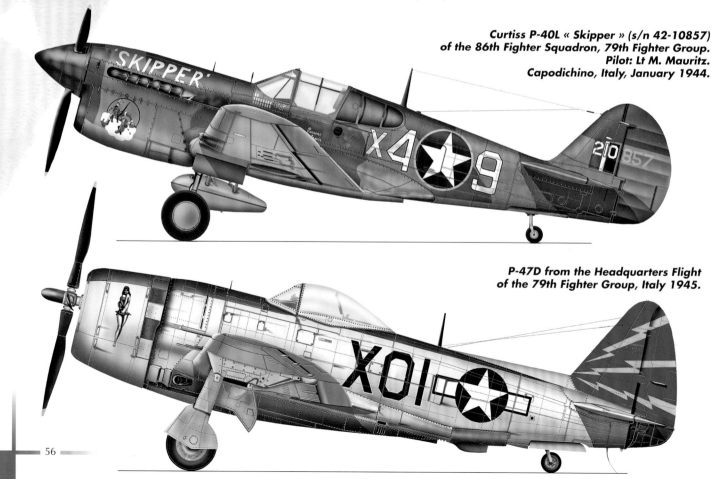

Curtiss P-40L « Skipper » (s/n 42-10857)
of the 86th Fighter Squadron, 79th Fighter Group.
Pilot: Lt M. Mauritz.
Capodichino, Italy, January 1944.

P-47D from the Headquarters Flight
of the 79th Fighter Group, Italy 1945.

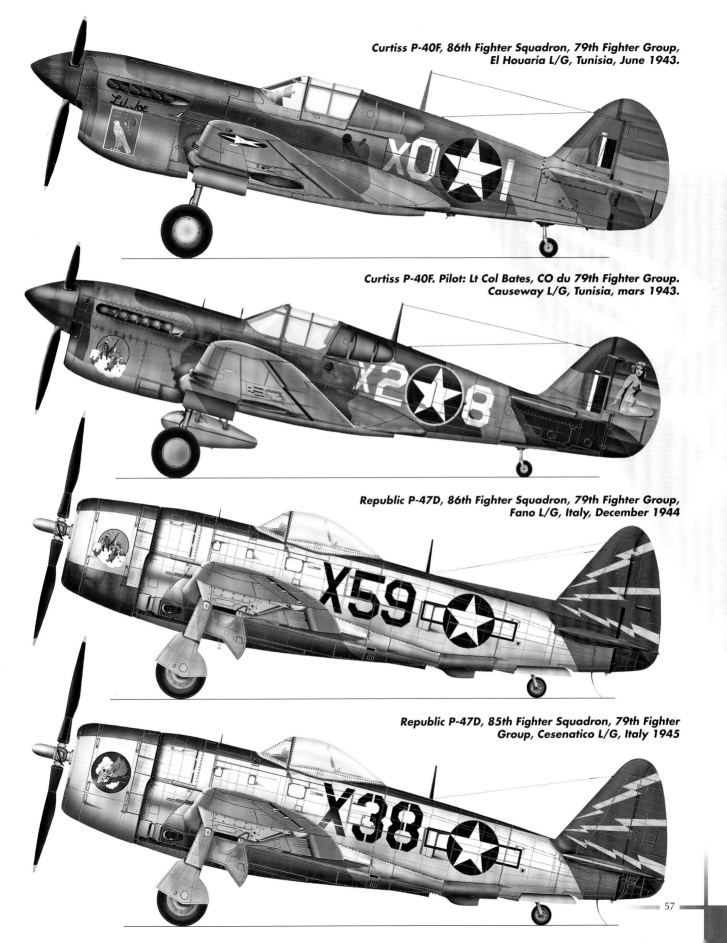

Curtiss P-40F, 86th Fighter Squadron, 79th Fighter Group, El Houaria L/G, Tunisia, June 1943.

Curtiss P-40F. Pilot: Lt Col Bates, CO du 79th Fighter Group. Causeway L/G, Tunisia, mars 1943.

Republic P-47D, 86th Fighter Squadron, 79th Fighter Group, Fano L/G, Italy, December 1944

Republic P-47D, 85th Fighter Squadron, 79th Fighter Group, Cesenatico L/G, Italy 1945

Pastoral scene in Italy, in 1944: a flock of sheep passes in front of some Republic P-47Ds from the 86th Fighter Squadron of the 79th Fighter Group. *(USAF)*

Republic P-47D, 86th Fighter Squadron, 79th Fighter Group, Cenenatico L/G, Italy, March 1945.

81ST FIGHTER GROUP

This group was assigned directly to the 12th Air Force in order to take part in Operation "Torch", the Allied landings in North Africa on 8 November 1942, but in which it was unable to take part since the pilots and planes only arrived in Morocco at the end of 1942. The 81st settled at Mediouna and started operations on 5 January 1943 with its P-39s. It was then transferred to various bases in Algeria and Tunisia to carry out patrols along the North-African coast from April to July 1943. During this period, it protected Allied convoys during the landings on Pantelleria and in Sicily.

In January 1944, the group, based at Montecorvino, Italy took part in getting ready for the Anzio Campaign before being assigned to India.

The 81st Fighter Group comprised three squadrons:
- **91st Fighter Squadron**: neither tactical code nor known distinctive colour.
- **92nd Fighter Squadron**: neither tactical code nor known distinctive colour.
- **93rd Fighter Squadron**: tactical code Q, but no known distinctive colour.

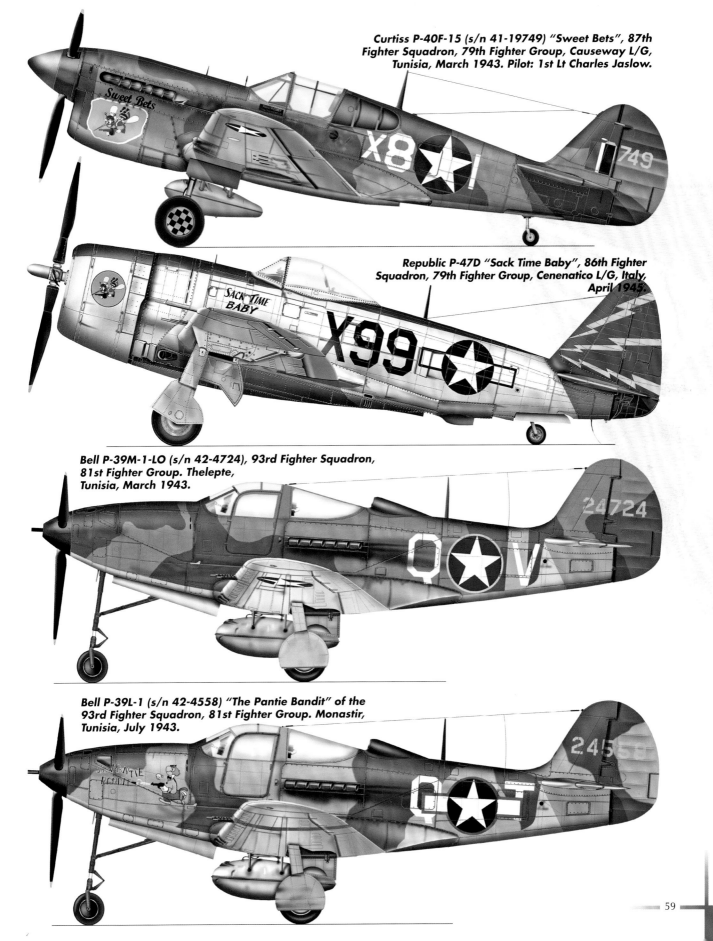

Curtiss P-40F-15 (s/n 41-19749) "Sweet Bets", 87th Fighter Squadron, 79th Fighter Group, Causeway L/G, Tunisia, March 1943. Pilot: 1st Lt Charles Jaslow.

Republic P-47D "Sack Time Baby", 86th Fighter Squadron, 79th Fighter Group, Cenenatico L/G, Italy, April 1945.

Bell P-39M-1-LO (s/n 42-4724), 93rd Fighter Squadron, 81st Fighter Group. Thelepte, Tunisia, March 1943.

Bell P-39L-1 (s/n 42-4558) "The Pantie Bandit" of the 93rd Fighter Squadron, 81st Fighter Group. Monastir, Tunisia, July 1943.

82TH FIGHTERGROUP

Created on 13 January 1942 under the name of the 82nd Pursuit Group (Interceptor) and activated on 9 February 1942, the group as renamed 82nd Fighter Group the following May and trained with P-38s. In September and October of the same year, it moved to Ireland to continue its training. In December it was sent to Telergma, Algeria and served in the 12th Air force until November 1943.

It took part in the Tunisian Campaign then in the landings on Pantelleria, during the conquest of Sicily and Italy. It operated against enemy air transport, carried out ground attack and bombing missions, escorted medium bombers during attacks on enemy shipping and carried out raids against Naples and Rome. It supported the ground troops directly during the invasion of Italy.

The group received a Distinguished Unit citation (DUC) for its ground support raid against enemy aircraft at Foggia, Italy on 25 August 1943 and received a second DUC for its action on 2 September 1943: while the group was escorting a formation of bombers attacking marshalling yards near Naples, it drove off strong opposition from enemy interceptors.

It was at San Pancrazo, Italy that the group settled in October 1943, before being assigned to the 15th Air Force the following November.

This group was made up of three squadrons:

- **95th Fighter Squadron** ("Boneheads"): tactical code "A", red distinctive colour.

- **96th Fighter Squadron**: tactical code "B", white distinctive colour for camouflaged aircraft and yellow for bare metal aircraft.

- **97th Fighter Squadron** ("Devil Cats"): tactical code "C", blue distinctive colour.

Lockheed P-38F-15 (s/n 43-2112) "Sad Sack", 95th Fighter Squadron, 82nd Fighter Group, Berteaux, Algeria, May 1943. Pilot: Captain Ernest K. Osher, CO of the 95th FS.

Lockheed P-38G-5 (s/n 42-12830) "Snooks IV", 95th Fighter Squadron, 82nd Fighter Group, Souk-el-Arba, Algeria, July 1943. Pilot: Lt William J. Sloan.

86TH FIGHTER GROUP

It was as a light bomber group that the 86th Fighter Group was created on 13 January 1942. It was activated on 10 February at Wills Field, Oklahoma then renamed the 86th Bombardment Group (Dive) on 13 January 1943 only to be renamed the 86th Fighter Bomber Group in August 1943. Finally the group was renamed the 86th Fighter Group in May 1944.

It was at Oran-la S2nia, Algeria, in May 1943 that the 86th joined the 12th Air Force and became operational in July of the same year, equipped with North American A-36 Apaches. Based at Korba, Tunisia, it took part in the invasion of Sicily and Southern Italy. From January to May 1944, the group was equipped with P-40s, planes which were replaced by P-47s while the Allies progressed towards Rome. Their targets included convoys, trains, shipping, ammunition dumps, troops supply depots, bridges and relays and rolling stock. They also carried out patrols and interdiction missions.

While stationed at Poretta, Corsica, the group covered the landings in Provence in August 1944. From December 1944 to April 1945, most of its operations concerned eliminating Axis lines of communication in Northern Italy. The 86th was also part of the 1st Tactical Air Force on 21 February 1945. After Italy, the group carried out missions against railways in Germany in April and May 1945.

During the period 1944-45, the 86th received two DUCs, the first for its action on 25 May 1944 when the group's planes had to face intensive AA fire while attacking German troops and vehicles trying to stop the Allied advance on Rome.

The second DUC was awarded for its action against German airfields and convoys in Northern Germany on 20 April 1945, thus disorganizing the German retreat in this zone. The 86th FG then remained in Germany as part of the occupation forces.

The group totalled 12 kills, all won with P-47s, and comprised three squadrons:

- **525th Fighter Squadron**: tactical code "A" on the A-36s, and tactical code from 1 to 39 on the P-47s; no colour attributed.

- **526th Fighter Squadron**: tactical code "B" on the A-36s, and tactical code from 40 to 69 on the P-47s; no colour attributed.

- **527th Fighter Squadron**: tactical code "C" on the A-36s, and tactical code from 70 to 99 on the P-47s; no colour attributed.

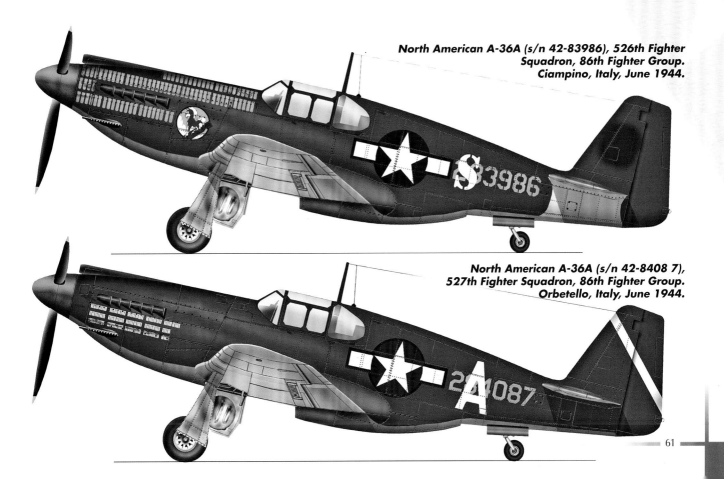

North American A-36A (s/n 42-83986), 526th Fighter Squadron, 86th Fighter Group. Ciampino, Italy, June 1944.

North American A-36A (s/n 42-8408 7), 527th Fighter Squadron, 86th Fighter Group. Orbetello, Italy, June 1944.

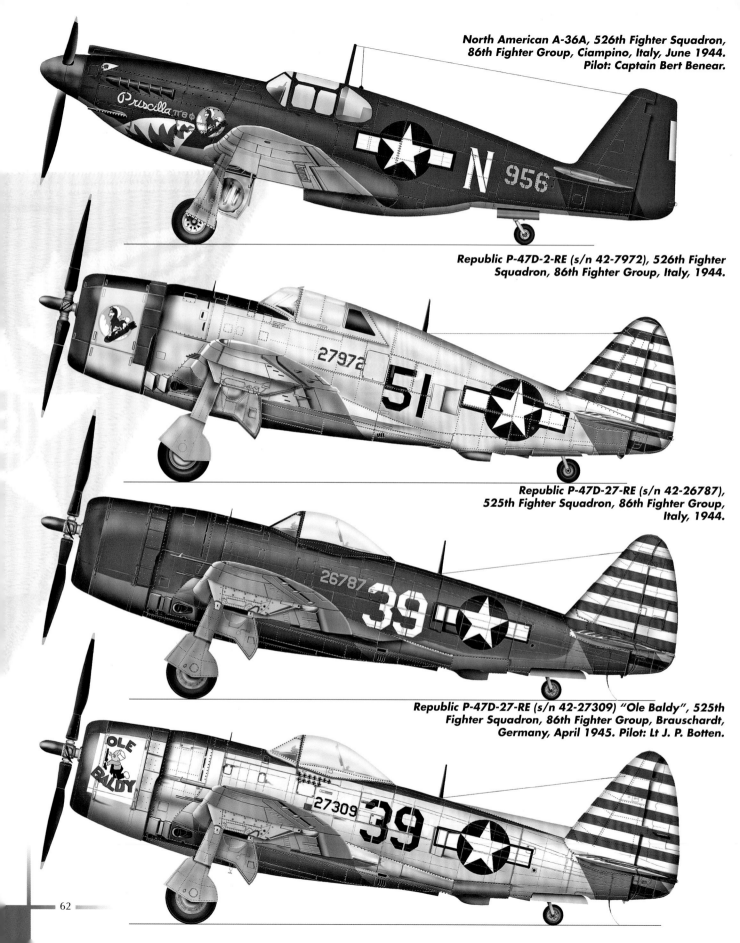

North American A-36A, 526th Fighter Squadron,
86th Fighter Group, Ciampino, Italy, June 1944.
Pilot: Captain Bert Benear.

Republic P-47D-2-RE (s/n 42-7972), 526th Fighter
Squadron, 86th Fighter Group, Italy, 1944.

Republic P-47D-27-RE (s/n 42-26787),
525th Fighter Squadron, 86th Fighter Group,
Italy, 1944.

Republic P-47D-27-RE (s/n 42-27309) "Ole Baldy", 525th
Fighter Squadron, 86th Fighter Group, Brauschardt,
Germany, April 1945. Pilot: Lt J. P. Botten.

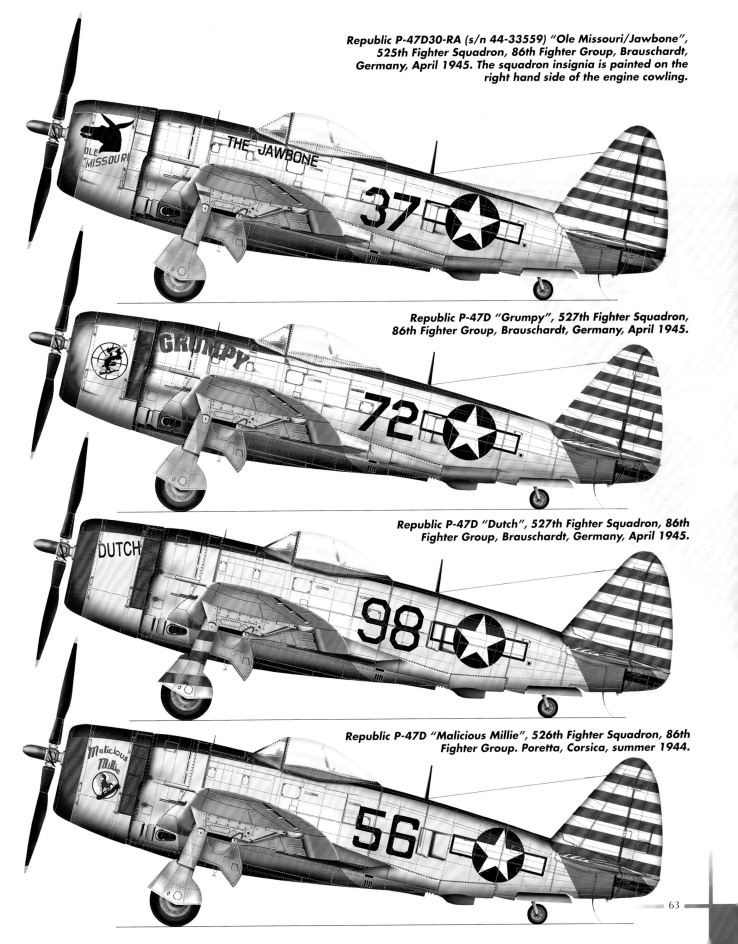

Republic P-47D30-RA (s/n 44-33559) "Ole Missouri/Jawbone",
525th Fighter Squadron, 86th Fighter Group, Brauschardt,
Germany, April 1945. The squadron insignia is painted on the
right hand side of the engine cowling.

Republic P-47D "Grumpy", 527th Fighter Squadron,
86th Fighter Group, Brauschardt, Germany, April 1945.

Republic P-47D "Dutch", 527th Fighter Squadron, 86th
Fighter Group, Brauschardt, Germany, April 1945.

Republic P-47D "Malicious Millie", 526th Fighter Squadron, 86th
Fighter Group. Poretta, Corsica, summer 1944.

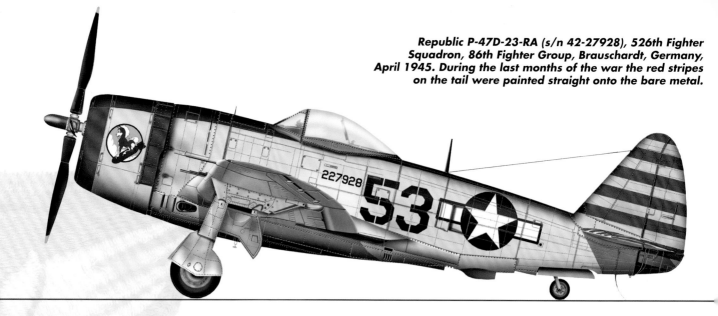

Republic P-47D-23-RA (s/n 42-27928), 526th Fighter Squadron, 86th Fighter Group, Brauschardt, Germany, April 1945. During the last months of the war the red stripes on the tail were painted straight onto the bare metal.

324TH FIGHTER GROUP

Created on 24 June 1942, the 324th Fighter Group was activated at Mitchell Field, New York on 6 July 1942 where it was issued with its P-40s. It was in the 9th Air Force that it started its operations in Egypt in October of the same year as soon as it was complete.

At the beginning of June 1943, the group settled at Kairouoan, then on other bases in Tunisia which it left in October 1943 when it was transferred to the 12th Air Force to pursue its operations from Cercola, Italy.

In its tactical role, it carried out strikes against road networks, railways, bridges, marshalling yards, supply depots, vehicles, artillery positions, troop concentrations and other targets.

In Italy, the 324th FG protected the Anzio landings in January 1944, before going over from P-40s to the P-47s the following July while it was based at Ghisonaccia, Corsica. It was declared fully operational on Thunderbolts during the landings in Provence in August.

The 324th FG supported the Allied forces during their progress towards Germany and at the end of 1944, set itself up at Dôle in the Jura then at Lunéville in January 1945, where it finished the war. It took part in reducing the Colmar bridgehead and covered the US VII Army's advance through the Siegfried Line in March 1945.

The group was awarded the French Croix de Guerre with Palms for having supported the French forces during their fighting in Italy and France. It ended the war with 29 kills to its credit.

Curtiss P-40F-1, 314th Fighter Squadron, 324th Fighter Group, El Kabrit, Egypt, March 1943. Pilot: 2nd Lt Andrew D'Antoni.

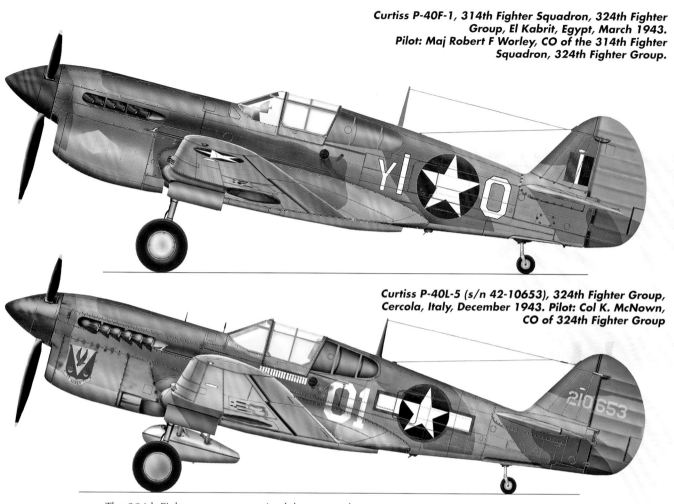

*Curtiss P-40F-1, 314th Fighter Squadron, 324th Fighter
Group, El Kabrit, Egypt, March 1943.
Pilot: Maj Robert F Worley, CO of the 314th Fighter
Squadron, 324th Fighter Group.*

*Curtiss P-40L-5 (s/n 42-10653), 324th Fighter Group,
Cercola, Italy, December 1943. Pilot: Col K. McNown,
CO of 324th Fighter Group*

The 324th Fighter group comprised three squadrons:

- **314th Fighter Squadron** ("The Hawks) tactical code on the P-40s from Y10 to Y39 and tactical code on the P-47s from 10 to 39; yellow distinctive colour.

- **315th Fighter Squadron** ("The Crusaders"): tactical code on the P-40s from Y40 to Y69 and tactical code on the P-47s from 40 to 69; red distinctive colour.

- **316th Fighter Squadron** ("Hell's Belles"): tactical code on the P-40s from Y70 to Y99 and tactical code on the P-47s from 70 to 99; yellow distinctive colour.

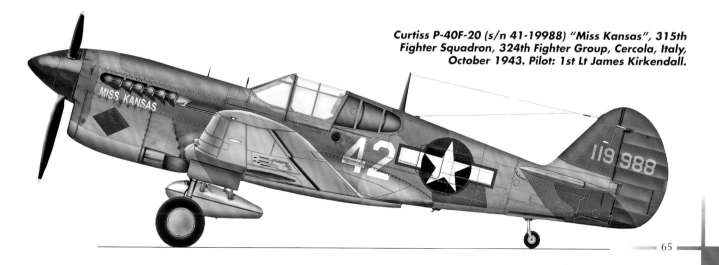

*Curtiss P-40F-20 (s/n 41-19988) "Miss Kansas", 315th
Fighter Squadron, 324th Fighter Group, Cercola, Italy,
October 1943. Pilot: 1st Lt James Kirkendall.*

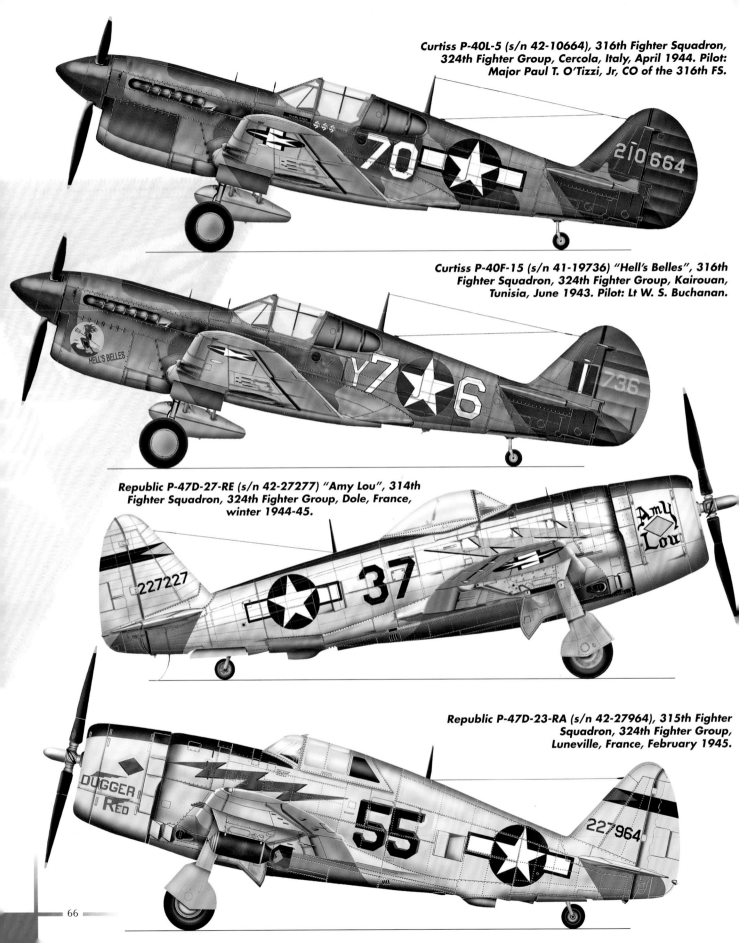

Curtiss P-40L-5 (s/n 42-10664), 316th Fighter Squadron, 324th Fighter Group, Cercola, Italy, April 1944. Pilot: Major Paul T. O'Tizzi, Jr, CO of the 316th FS.

Curtiss P-40F-15 (s/n 41-19736) "Hell's Belles", 316th Fighter Squadron, 324th Fighter Group, Kairouan, Tunisia, June 1943. Pilot: Lt W. S. Buchanan.

Republic P-47D-27-RE (s/n 42-27277) "Amy Lou", 314th Fighter Squadron, 324th Fighter Group, Dole, France, winter 1944-45.

Republic P-47D-23-RA (s/n 42-27964), 315th Fighter Squadron, 324th Fighter Group, Luneville, France, February 1945.

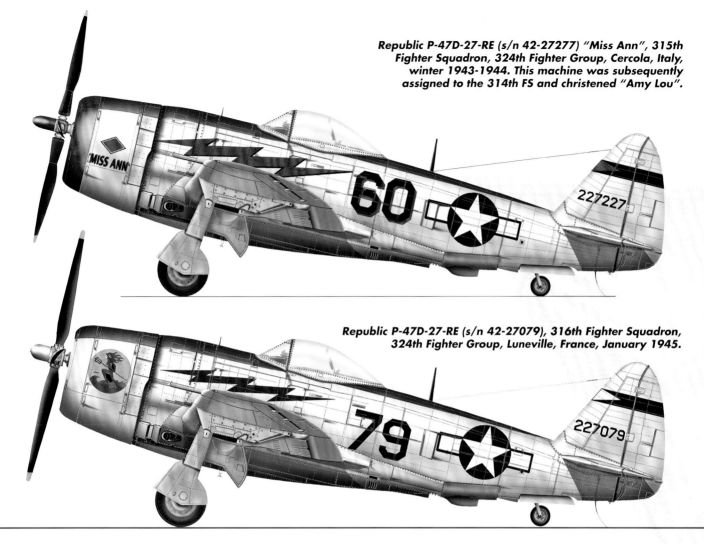

Republic P-47D-27-RE (s/n 42-27277) "Miss Ann", 315th Fighter Squadron, 324th Fighter Group, Cercola, Italy, winter 1943-1944. This machine was subsequently assigned to the 314th FS and christened "Amy Lou".

Republic P-47D-27-RE (s/n 42-27079), 316th Fighter Squadron, 324th Fighter Group, Luneville, France, January 1945.

325TH FIGHTER GROUP

It was at Mitchell Field, New York that the 325th Fighter Group was created on 24 June 1942 and activated the following 3 August. It trained on P-40s before embarking aboard the *USS Ranger* heading to North Africa at the beginning of 1943 to take part in the African Campaign. Its planes took off from the carrier to go to Casablanca, Morocco on 19 January 1943 where the group was assigned to the 12th Air force.

On 17 April 1943, the 325th FG started fighting, escorting bombers and carrying out sea patrols from Algeria and Tunisia. It took part in the defeat of the Axis forces in Tunisia, the reduction of Pantelleria and the conquest of Sicily.

The group was awarded a Distinguished Unit Citation for its action in Sardinia where it destroyed a large number of enemy aircraft. From September to October 1943 the group proceeded with its conversion onto P-47s and went over to the 15th Air force in November 1943 while it was based at Soliman, Tunisia.

The 325th Fighter Group had three squadrons:
- **317th Fighter Squadron**: tactical code from 10 to 39, yellow distinctive colour.
- **318th Fighter Squadron**: tactical code from 40 to 69, white distinctive colour.
- **319th Fighter Squadron**: tactical code from 70 to 99, red distinctive colour.

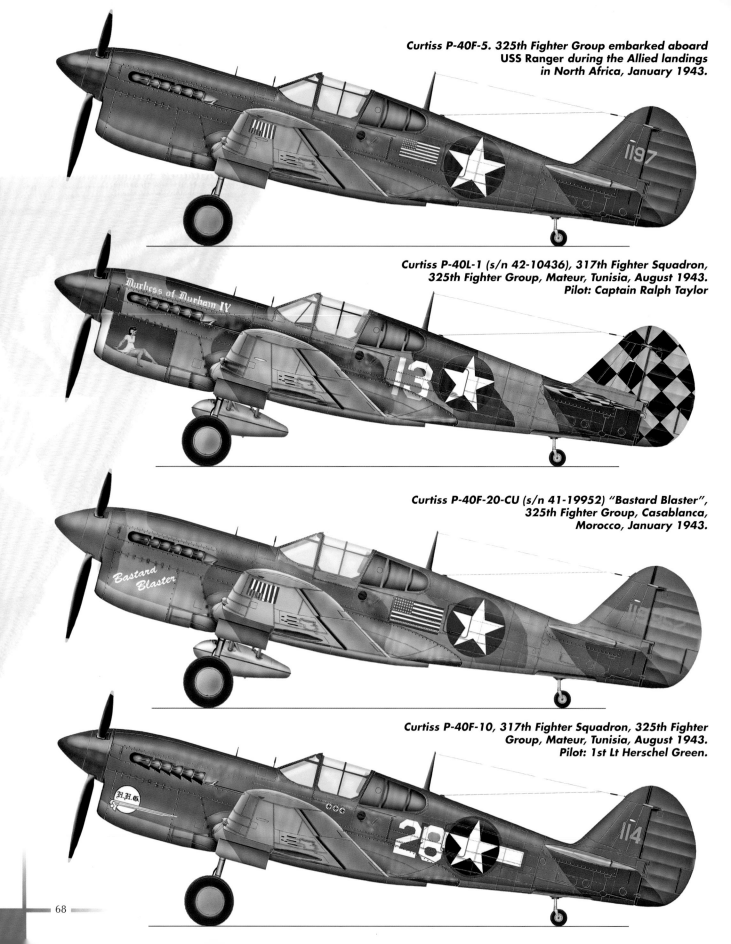

Curtiss P-40F-5. 325th Fighter Group embarked aboard USS Ranger during the Allied landings in North Africa, January 1943.

Curtiss P-40L-1 (s/n 42-10436), 317th Fighter Squadron, 325th Fighter Group, Mateur, Tunisia, August 1943. Pilot: Captain Ralph Taylor

Curtiss P-40F-20-CU (s/n 41-19952) "Bastard Blaster", 325th Fighter Group, Casablanca, Morocco, January 1943.

Curtiss P-40F-10, 317th Fighter Squadron, 325th Fighter Group, Mateur, Tunisia, August 1943. Pilot: 1st Lt Herschel Green.

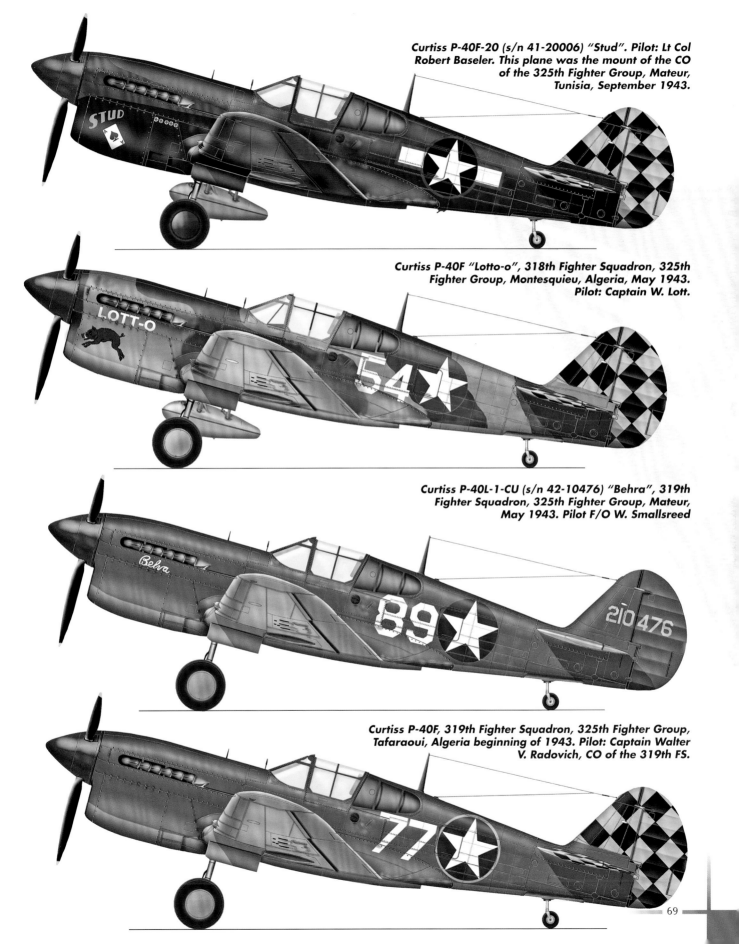

Curtiss P-40F-20 (s/n 41-20006) "Stud". Pilot: Lt Col Robert Baseler. This plane was the mount of the CO of the 325th Fighter Group, Mateur, Tunisia, September 1943.

Curtiss P-40F "Lotto-o", 318th Fighter Squadron, 325th Fighter Group, Montesquieu, Algeria, May 1943. Pilot: Captain W. Lott.

Curtiss P-40L-1-CU (s/n 42-10476) "Behra", 319th Fighter Squadron, 325th Fighter Group, Mateur, May 1943. Pilot F/O W. Smallsreed

Curtiss P-40F, 319th Fighter Squadron, 325th Fighter Group, Tafaraoui, Algeria beginning of 1943. Pilot: Captain Walter V. Radovich, CO of the 319th FS.

350TH FIGHTER GROUP

It was on 2 October 1942 while in the 8th Air Force that the 350th fighter Group as activated while based at Bushey Hall, Great Britain. The group reached North Africa gradually from January to February 1943 and various elements were deployed in North Africa on the numerous airfields in Algeria and Tunisia.

It was assigned to the 12th Air Force for the whole war, flying Bell P-39s and P-40s and a few Lockheed P-38 Lightnings before converting to Republic P-47s in August and September 1944 while it was based at Ajaccio, Corsica.

The 350th Fighter Group carried out patrols and interceptions while protecting the convoys and supported the ground forces along the Algerian coast. It ended its operations in North Africa during the Tunisian Campaign in May 1943. When Sicily fell in July 1943, the 350th FG moved

*Above. **During a ground attack mission in the Brescia region of Italy, a flak shell cut the oil supply of P-47D belonging to 1st Lt. Edwin L. King, 350th FG. With his "Jug", mostly covered in oil and with an opaque cockpit canopy, the pilot managed to land without damage on his airfield. The 347th's squadron insignia has been painted on the engine cowling.**
(USAF)*

to Sardinia to take part in the Italian Campaign. It was awarded a Distinguished Unit Citation for having carried out ten missions on 6 April 1944 and, in spite of intense AA fire and a lot of attacks by enemy interceptors, for striking troop concentrations, bridges, vehicles, barracks and radar installations. It also covered the Allied landings on the Island of Elba in June 1944 then, based in Corsica, it supported the landings in Provence in August 1944.

It was at Pisa, Italy that the 350th FG ended the war then it returned to the States in July-August 1945.

The three squadrons making up the 350th Fighter Group were the 345th, 346th and 347th.

Bell P-39N-1 (s/n 42-18322), 345th Fighter Squadron, 350th Fighter Group, Cagliari, Sardinia, November 1943.

The group adopted an unusual code for its P-47s: the first character represented the last number of the squadron, the second character was a letter indicating the flight in the squadron and the third character was the individual number of the machine in the Flight.

The markings of the 345th Fighter Squadron was made up of a flash of lightning on a dark blue stripe painted on the tail. The planes of the 346th had a black and white checkerboard tail whereas those in the 347th had a big red letter A on the tail.

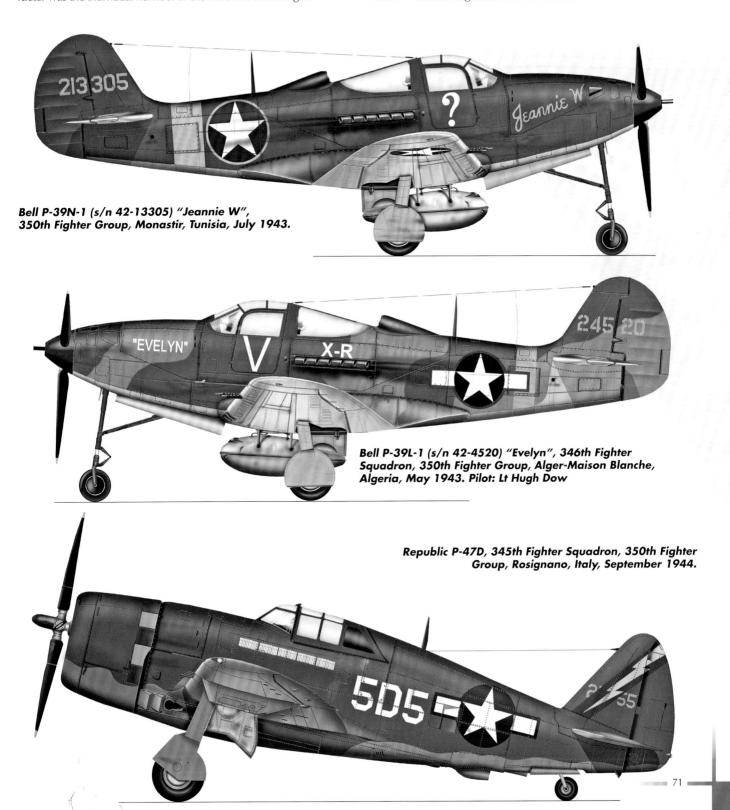

**Bell P-39N-1 (s/n 42-13305) "Jeannie W",
350th Fighter Group, Monastir, Tunisia, July 1943.**

**Bell P-39L-1 (s/n 42-4520) "Evelyn", 346th Fighter
Squadron, 350th Fighter Group, Alger-Maison Blanche,
Algeria, May 1943. Pilot: Lt Hugh Dow**

**Republic P-47D, 345th Fighter Squadron, 350th Fighter
Group, Rosignano, Italy, September 1944.**

A formation of Republic P-47D Thunderbolts from the 345th Fighter Squadron, 350th Fighter Group, over Italy in 1945. In the centre P-47D-27-RE s/n 42-27260 "Flak Happy". *(USAF)*

Republic P-47D-27-RE (s/n 42-27260) "Flak Happy", 345th Fighter Squadron, 350th Fighter Group, Pisa, Italy, March -April 1945.

Republic P-47D-15-RE (s/n 42-275809), 346th Fighter Squadron, 350th Fighter Group, Italy, end of 194

Republic P-47D-27-RE (s/n 42-27068) "Bach's Boche Bustin Bastard", 346th Fighter Squadron, 350th Fighter Group, Pisa, Italy, March-April 1945.

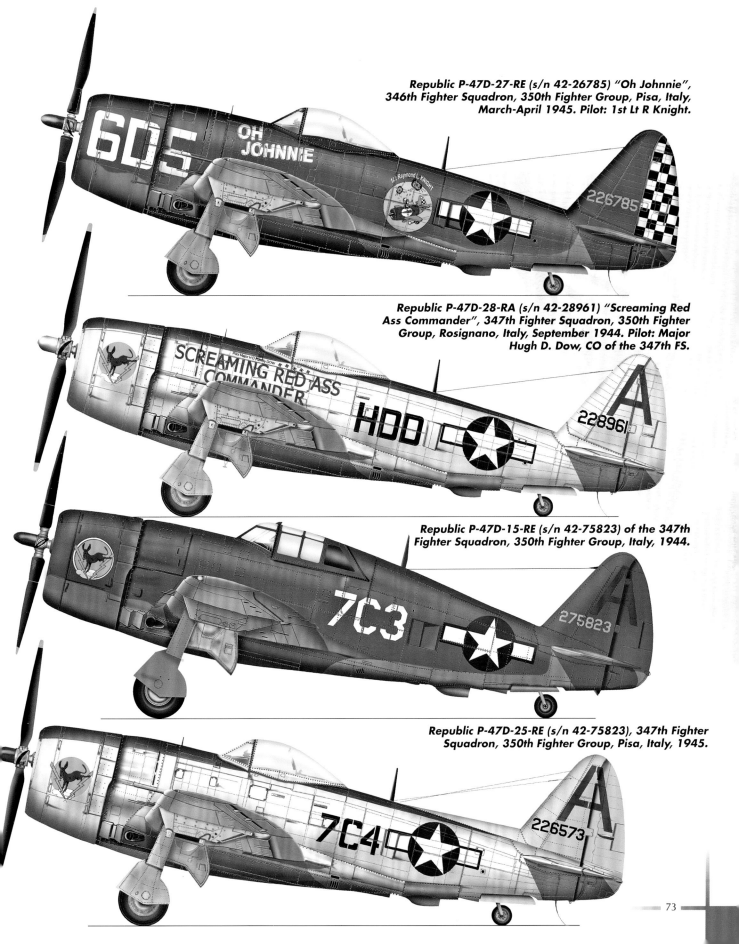

Republic P-47D-27-RE (s/n 42-26785) "Oh Johnnie",
346th Fighter Squadron, 350th Fighter Group, Pisa, Italy,
March-April 1945. Pilot: 1st Lt R Knight.

Republic P-47D-28-RA (s/n 42-28961) "Screaming Red
Ass Commander", 347th Fighter Squadron, 350th Fighter
Group, Rosignano, Italy, September 1944. Pilot: Major
Hugh D. Dow, CO of the 347th FS.

Republic P-47D-15-RE (s/n 42-75823) of the 347th
Fighter Squadron, 350th Fighter Group, Italy, 1944.

Republic P-47D-25-RE (s/n 42-75823), 347th Fighter
Squadron, 350th Fighter Group, Pisa, Italy, 1945.

1ST BRAZILIAN FIGHTER SQUADRON

The Brazilian 1° Grupo de Aviacão de Caça arrived in Italy on 6 August 1944 and was attached to the 350th Fighter Group as its fourth squadron under the name of the 1st Brazilian Fighter Squadron or 1st BFS. Equipped with P-47s, it was based at Tarquinia, Italy and took part n the Italian Campaign, carrying out the same missions as the other three squadrons in the Group, The 1st BFS carried out 184 missions in the 350th Fighter Group,

Opposite.
Two Republic P-47D-25-REs (s/n 42-26755 and 42-26756), 1st BFS (Brazilian Fighter Squadron/1° Grupo de Aviacão de Caça, (GAVCA) in Italy, 1945.
(USAF)

Republic P-47D-25-RE (s/n 42-26756), 1st BFS (Brazilian Fighter Squadron /1° Grupo de Aviacão de Caça, GAVCA). Pisa, Italy, 1945.

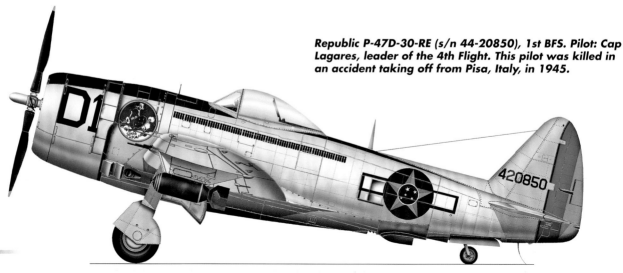

Republic P-47D-30-RE (s/n 44-20850), 1st BFS. Pilot: Cap Lagares, leader of the 4th Flight. This pilot was killed in an accident taking off from Pisa, Italy, in 1945.

THE 12TH AIR FORCE'S
NIGHT FIGHTER SQUADRONS

414TH NIGHT FIGHTER SQUADRON

This squadron was activated on 26 January 1943 and attached to the 12th Air Force from the following 10 May until the end of the war. Equipped with Bristol Beaufighter Mk VIFs, it was based at Oran-la Senia, Algeria. In 1943, it operated on the Mediterranean front, in Algeria, Tunisia and Sardinia and then on 9 January 1944, it settled on the base at Ghisonaccia and Borgo, Corsica. In the autumn of the same year, it moved to Pisa, Italy and was issued equipped Northrop P-61 Black Widows at the end of 1944.

The 414th obtained five kills against German aircraft and was awarded a DUC for its action on 23 and 24 January 1944.

Neither tactical code nor distinctive colours.

415TH NIGHT FIGHTER SQUADRON

The 415th was activated on 8 February 1943. Attached to the 12th Air Force, it settled at Oran-la Senia, Algeria on 12 May 1943 with its Beaufighter Mk VIFs, which it kept until April 1945. In 1943, it frequently changed airfields in Tunisia, Sicily and Italy in order to take part in the various Allied operations carried out on the Mediterranean front.

It settled at Solenzara, Corsica in July 1944 and took part in the landings in Provence. Its first base in Metropolitan France was le Vallon in September 1944. In April 1945, the 415th NFS went over to P-61 Black Widows and finished the war on the airfield at Braunschardt, Germany.

Neither tactical code nor distinctive colours.

416TH NIGHT FIGHTER SQUADRON

The 416th was activated on 20 February 1943 and attached to the 12th Air Force from the following 8 August. This squadron was equipped with Beaufighter Mk VIFs and Mosquito NF30s. Based initially at Alger, it then left for Bizerte, Tunisia, in September 1943 in order to cover operations in the Mediterranean theatre. It moved to Lecce, Italy on the 27th and often changed airfields in the Peninsula. On 14 August 1944, it left for Borgo, Corsica to take part in the landings in Provence and in September it returned to Northern Italy from where it carried on with its operations until the end of the war.

Neither tactical code nor distinctive colours.

417TH NIGHT FIGHTER SQUADRON

It was on 20 February 1943 that the 417th Night Fighter Squadron was activated. Equipped with Beaufighter Mk VIFs; it settled at Tafaraoui, Algeria on 8 August 1943 to be incorporated into the 12th Air Force. In September 1944, it moved to Borgo, Corsica to protect the Allied advance up the Rhone Valley. In March 1945 it converted to P-61 Black Widows and carried on with its missions until the end of the war.

Neither tactical code nor distinctive colours.

Northrop P-61B 42-39684, of the 416th Night Fighter Squadron flying over Italy in 1945. (USAF)

Bristol Beaufighter Mk VIF, 416th Night Fighter Squadron, Elmas, Sardinia, November 1943.

PATSY

KV912

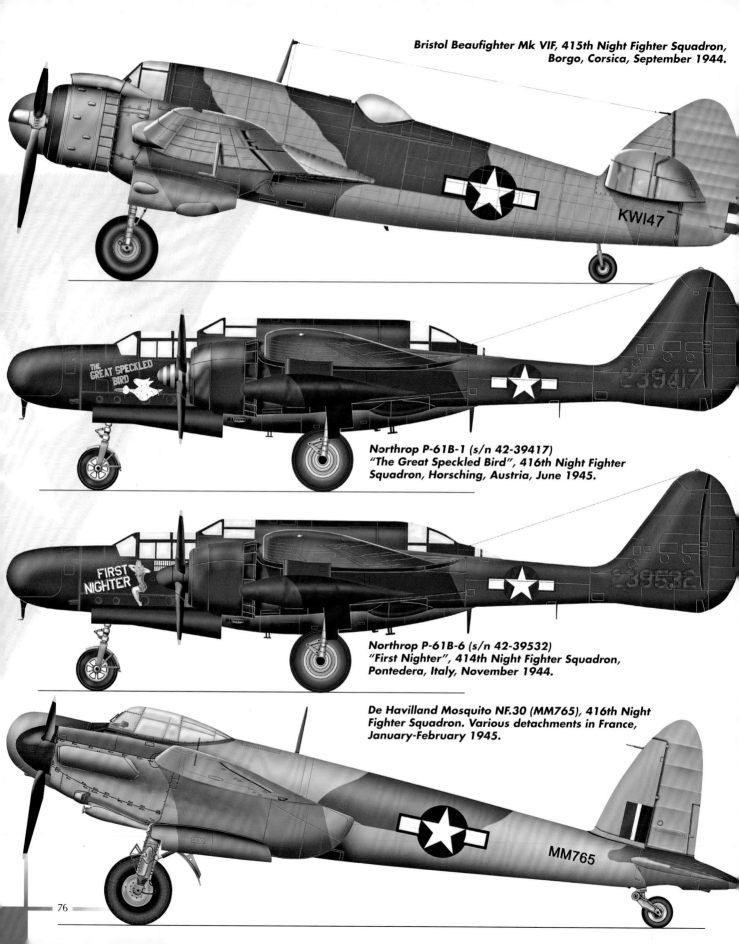

Bristol Beaufighter Mk VIF, 415th Night Fighter Squadron, Borgo, Corsica, September 1944.

KW147

Northrop P-61B-1 (s/n 42-39417) "The Great Speckled Bird", 416th Night Fighter Squadron, Horsching, Austria, June 1945.

THE GREAT SPECKLED BIRD

239417

Northrop P-61B-6 (s/n 42-39532) "First Nighter", 414th Night Fighter Squadron, Pontedera, Italy, November 1944.

FIRST NIGHTER

239532

De Havilland Mosquito NF.30 (MM765), 416th Night Fighter Squadron. Various detachments in France, January-February 1945.

MM765

Servicing Bristol Beaufighter Mk VIF "Honeychile", 414th NFS at night on the airfield at Grottaglie, Italy, in 1944. In the background are some Lockheed Hudsons wearing Coastal Command-type camouflage. (USAF)

FRANCE

BORDEAUX

"F
JUNE 19

SPAIN
(neutral)

MADRID ■

BALEAR

PORTUGAL
(neutral)

■ LISBON

CENTER TASK FORCE
8 NOVEMBER 1942

WESTERN TASK FORCE
8 NOVEMBER 1942

GIBRALTAR

SPANISH MOROCCO

ORAN

PORT-LYAUTEY
MAZAGAN ■ RABBAT
CASABLANCA

SAFI

MOROCCO

SWITZERLAND
(neutral)

ITALY

CROATIA

LYON

..NE"
..MBER 1942

SAINT-TROPEZ OPERATIONS
"ANVIL/DRAGOON"
15 AUGUST 1944

MARSEILLE

CORSE

LIBERATION OF ROMA
4 JUNE 1944

SALERNO
OPERATION "AVALANCHE"
9-16 SEPTEMBER 1943

ANZIO
OPERATION "SHINGLE"
22 JANUARY 1944

NAPLES

SARDINIA

..LANDS

..ASTERN TASK FORCE
NOVEMBER 1942 - MAY 1943

PALERMO

INVASION OF SICILY
OPERATION "HUSKY"
9 JULY - 17 AUGUST 1942

BIZERTE

BONE

TUNIS
1943

MALTA
(Great-Britain)

BOUGIE

..LGER

CONSTANTINE

KASSERINE PASS
19-25 FEBRUARY 1943

BISKRA

SFAX

MARETH
1943

TRIPOLI

ALGERIA

TUNISIA

LIBYA

15TH AIR FORCE

The 15th Air Force was started on 1 November 1943 in order to operate on the Mediterranean Front (MTO), with its groups being based mainly on airfields in Southern Italy. Its main objectives were enemy oil refineries and aircraft factories.

*Above. **A formation of B-24 Liberators from the 15th AF flying over the Ploesti oil refineries (Rumania) during Operation Tidal Wave which was one of the group's main feats of arms.** (USAF)*

*Below. **A box of B-17s from the 15th AF caught in flak while bombing Debreczen, Hungary on 21 September 1944.** (USAF)*

MAKE UP OF 15TH AIR FORCE WAS MADE UP IN NOVEMBER 1943	
FIGHTERS	
GROUPS	TYPES OF PLANES
1st FG	P-38
14th FG	P-38
82nd FG	P-38
325th FG	P-47
BOMBERS	
GROUPS	TYPES OF PLANES
2nd BG	B-17
97th BG	B-17
98th BG	B-24
99th BG	B-17
301st BG	B-17
376th BG	B-24

MAKE UP OF 15TH AIR FORCE WAS MADE UP IN 1944-45	
FIGHTERS	
GROUPS	TYPES OF PLANES
1st FG	P-38
14th FG	P-38
31st FG	P-51
52nd FG	P-51
82nd FG	P-38
325th FG	P-47 puis P-51
332nd FG	P-47 puis P-51
BBOMBERS	
GROUPS	TYPES OF PLANES
2nd BG	B-17
97th BG	B-17
98th BG	B-24
99th BG	B-17
301st BG	B-17
376th BG	B-24
449th BG	B-24
450th BG	B-24
451st BG	B-24
454th BG	B-24
455th BG	B-24
456th BG	B-24
459th BG	B-24
460th BG	B-24
461st BG	B-24
463rd BG	B-17
464th BG	B-243
465th BG	B-24
483rd BG	B-17
484th BG	B-24
485th BG	B-24

The 15th AF dropped more than 300 000 tons of bombs on targets in twelve European countries, with its heavy bombers carrying out 148 955 sorties and its fighters 87 732. It lost 3 364 planes and 21 671 of its men were killed, wounded or listed as missing among whom 20 430 were bomber crews and 1 187 fighter pilots.

MAIN OBJECTIVE: THE REFINERIES!

At the end of the bombing campaign, enemy refining activity had been reduced by 30 to 40% and during the period from April to August 1944, average production was reduced by 60%.

During the last months of the conflict, the 15th AF continued its attacks by dropping 10 000 tons of bombs on three synthetic petrol factories in Silesia and another in Poland, thereby reducing the whole of their production by 20% in February 1945 compared to what it had been in June the previous year. Moreover, after the devastating attacks against the Wiener-Neustadt and Regensburg industrial complexes where German fighters were being built, estimated production dropped from 650 to 250 fighters.

Opposite.
B-24 Liberators from the 450th Bomb Group of 15th AF going though an AAA barrage while on a bombing mission against the port installations at Toulon, on 29 April 1944.
(USAF)

Above. **Destroying the Axis fuel industry complexes was one of the main missions assigned to the 15th AF. Here a Liberator is flying over the clouds of smoke caused by burning refineries in Budapest.** (USAF

Above. **Major General Nathan Farragut Twining (left) congratulating Colonel Robert Eaton, CO of the 451st BG for the second DUC awarded to this group, this time for the Ploesti raid in April 1944. After serving in the Pacific, Twining commanded the 15th AF from November 1943, replacing James H. Doolittle. At the end of the war, he was briefly sent to the Pacific to command the 20th AF until Japan capitulated in August 1945.** (USAF)

Below. **Four P-38Ls from the 27th FS of the 1st FG banking in the Italian sky in 1944.** (USAF)

PHOTO RECONNAISSANCE	
GROUPS	TYPE OF PLANES
5th PRG	F-5 Lightning
SQUADRONS	
154th Weather Reco	P-38
859th Bomb Sqdn (H) (S)	B-24 (1945)
885th Bomb Sqdn (H) (S)	B-24

THE 15TH AIR FORCE'S ACES
WITH MORE THAN 10 KILLS

NAME	GROUP	NUMBER OF KILLS
John Voll	31st	21
Herschel Green	325th	18
James S. Varnell	52nd	17
Samuel J. Brown	31st	15
Robert C. Curtis	52nd	14
James L. Brooks	31st	13
Harry A. Parker	325th	13
Mickael Brezas	14th	12
Norman C. Skogstad	31st	12
William Leverette	14th	11
Robert J. Goebel	31st	11
Charles M. McCorkle	31st	11

Above. **A P-51 taking off from an Italian airfield whose runways have been covered with PSP matting. From 1944 onwards the Mustang was the main 15th AF fighter with its range – extended thanks to two under-wing drop tanks visible here – enabling it to escort the heavy bombers deep into enemy territory.**

SUPPORT FOR THE ALLIES

The 15th Air Force also supported the Allies troops by bombing targets during the battle for Anzio, Monte-Cassino and Rome. One of the unexpected aspects of the 15th AF's operations was saving and evacuating crews shot down over enemy territory, evacuation operations which were carried out by no other US Air Force. During more than 300 of these missions, the 15th AF brought back prisoners of war from Tunisia, Italy, France, Switzerland and Greece, Albania, Bulgaria, Rumania, Hungary, Yugoslavia, Austria and Germany.

The 15th Air Force was disbanded on 15 September 1945.

Opposite. **Captain John J. Voll aboard "American Beauty", P-51 "HL-B", visible in the background, leading a patrol of four Mustangs from the 308th FS (31st FG). Voll was one of the 15th AF's "ace of aces" with his 21 confirmed kills.**
(USAF)

Above.
Flying Fortresses from the 15th AF en route to Sofia, Bulgaria, flying over the Balkans. In the foreground is "Hustlin' Huzzy", B-17F-95-BO s/n 42-30267 from the 414th BS (97th BG) which was shot down over Bucharest on 23 June 1944 by Rumanian Fighters.
(USAF)

Opposite.
A formation of 15th AF B-26 Marauders seen from an unusual angle. This twin engined bomber was the main medium bomber in this Air Force. *(USAF)*

Opposite.
A 15th Air Force Boeing B-17 flying over the airfield at Kalamaki, near Athens, blacked out by the columns of smoke caused by the bombs. During this mission which took place on 15 September 1944, more than a dozen of these four-engined planes were shot down.
(USAF)

Bellow.
"Heavy outdoor maintenance work" on a P-51B from the **308th FS (31st FG)** on the airfield at San Severo, Foggia, Italy, April 1944.
(USAF)

Returning from escorting bombers over Austria, a large formation of P-38s make a low-level fly past over their base. The Lightning was the 15th AF's main escort fighter before being gradually replaced by the P-51 which had a longer range and was less delicate to fly.(USAF)

The 15th AF was the only US Army Air Force to have a unit entirely made up of Afro-American personnel. The 332nd FG was nicknamed the "Tuskegee Airmen" after the place where it was formed. In front of "Skipper's Darlin' III", P-51C (s/n° 42-103960) belonging to Captain Andrew "Jug" Turner, are from left to right: Lieutenant Dempsey W. Morgan, Lieutenant Carroll S. Woods, Lieutenant Robert H. Nelson Jr, Captain Andrew D. Turner, CO of the 100th FS, and Lieutenant Clarence D. Lester (3 confirmed kills). (USAF)

Opposite.
**Staff Sergeant
Alfred D. Morris
helps Captain
William T. Mattison,
Operations Officer
of the 100th FS of
the 332nd FG into
his Mustang. Both
men's names have
been painted under
the windshield.**
(USAF)

Below.
**"Sweet Sue", P-38J
s/n 43-28650 from
the 27th FS (1st FG)
in flight over Italy
in 1944.**
(USAF)

P-51s from the "Tuskegee Airmen" (332nd FG) doing a low-level fly-past over their Italian base in 1944. (USAF)

"Gum Drop/Patches", a Liberator from the 781st BS of the 465th BG drops its bombs on the port installations at Forli on 19 May 1944. This B-24H-15-FO built by Ford (s/n 42-52449) was shot down by enemy fighter over Ploesti (Rumania) on 6 June 1944 and its ten crewmen taken prisoner. (USAF)

Weather conditions were not always favourable in Italy. Here P-47s from the 325th FG ("Checkertail Clan") on a soaking airfield. *(USAF)*

Escorted by P-38 Lightnings, these 15th AF B-17 Flying Fortresses are heading for their target, Augsburg, in Germany on 27 February 1945. *(USAF)*

15TH AIR FORCE'S BOMBER GROUPS

Both types of heavy bomber used by the 15th AF can be seen on this shot. In the foreground is B-24L-10-FO Liberator s/n 44-49647 from the 724th BS (451st BG) alongside B-17G-60-DL Flying Fortress s/n 44-6643 from the 96th BS (2nd BG) which crashed during a training mission December 1944, after carrying out 17 combat sorties. (USAF)

2ND BOMBARDMENT GROUP (HEAVY)

This heavy bomber group was transferred from the 12th Air Force to the 15th in November 1943 and moved to the airfield at Amendola near Foggia, Italy in December 1943. From there it carried out 331 missions using B-17s until May 1945 and lost 176 machines in combat during of the war. Its last war mission was on 1 May 1945 against a marshalling yard at Salzburg, Austria. The 2nd Bombardment Group (Heavy) was made up of four squadrons. From January 1945 on, the planes wore a dark blue stripe on their wings.
— **20th Bomb Squadron (H)**, no distinctive colour.
— **49th Bomb Squadron (H)**, no distinctive colour.
— **96th Bomb Squadron (H)**, no distinctive colour.
— **429th Bomb Squadron (H)**, no distinctive colour.
For the tactical symbols see the profiles.

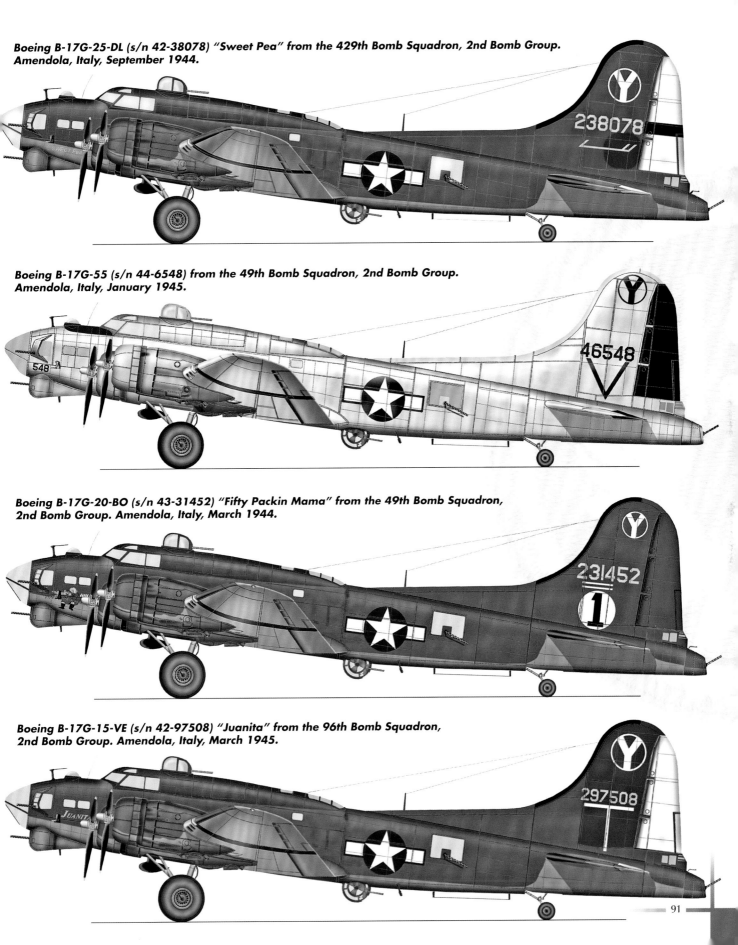

Boeing B-17G-25-DL (s/n 42-38078) "Sweet Pea" from the 429th Bomb Squadron, 2nd Bomb Group. Amendola, Italy, September 1944.

Boeing B-17G-55 (s/n 44-6548) from the 49th Bomb Squadron, 2nd Bomb Group. Amendola, Italy, January 1945.

Boeing B-17G-20-BO (s/n 43-31452) "Fifty Packin Mama" from the 49th Bomb Squadron, 2nd Bomb Group. Amendola, Italy, March 1944.

Boeing B-17G-15-VE (s/n 42-97508) "Juanita" from the 96th Bomb Squadron, 2nd Bomb Group. Amendola, Italy, March 1945.

97TH BOMBARDMENT GROUP (HEAVY)

In November 1943 the 97th Bombardment Group (Heavy), based at Depienne in Tunisia was transferred from the 12th Air Force to the 15th with its B-17s. From November 1943 to April 1945, it carried out mainly long distance missions against targets situated in Western and Central Europe, attacking oil refineries, aircraft factories, and marshalling yards as well as other strategic targets.

In January 1944 it was stationed on the airfield at Amendola, Italy and remained there until the end of the war. In order to support the Allied forces at Anzio and Monte Cassino, it struck at enemy communications as well as transport networks and airfields. It also bombed the coastal defences in preparation for the Provence landings and supported the US Vth Army and the British VIIIth Army as they worked their way up towards Northern Italy. The group was awarded the Distinguished Unit citation (DUC) for having bombed an aircraft factory at Steyr, Austria on 24 February 1944 during the "Big Week". This intensive air campaign, which took place from 20 to 25 February against the German aircraft industry, used more than a thousand bombers from the 8th and the 15th Air Forces.

The 97th was awarded a second DUC after a raid against one of the Ploesti refineries in Rumania on 18 August 1944. The group lost 124 B-17s in combat during the war and was disbanded in Italy on 29 October 1945.

The 97th Bombardment Group (H) was made up of four squadrons:

- **340th Bomb Squadron (H).** Letter "Y" in a white triangle on the tail (the 97th BG marking) and tactical code represented by the figure "0". During the last weeks of the war this squadron bore a red checkerboard on a metal background on the rudder.

- **341st Bomb Squadron (H).** Letter "Y" in a white triangle on the tail (the 97th BG marking) and tactical code represented by the figure "1". During the last weeks of the war this squadron bore a red checkerboard on a metal background on the rudder.

- **342nd Bomb Squadron (H).** Letter "Y" in a white triangle on the tail (the 97th BG marking) and tactical code represented by the figure "2". During the last weeks of the war this squadron bore slanting red stripes on the rudder.

- **414th Bomb Squadron (H).** Letter "Y" in a white triangle on the tail (the 97th BG marking) and tactical code represented by the figure "4". During the last weeks of the war this squadron bore slanting red stripes on the rudder.

Above. **This B-17G-50-DL (s/n 44-6442) from the 340th BS of the 97th BG seen here in flight returning from a mission, was shot down over Kalamaki, Greece on 21 January 1945.** *(USAF)*

Below. **A group of Soviet officers watch "Idiot's Delight" (B-17G-60-BO s/n 42-102918) from the 324th BS taking off. This was the first 15th AF bomber to carry out a shuttle mission on 26 May 1944, transiting in the USSR between two missions. This Flying Fortress was lost the following month during a raid against Munich.** *(USAF)*

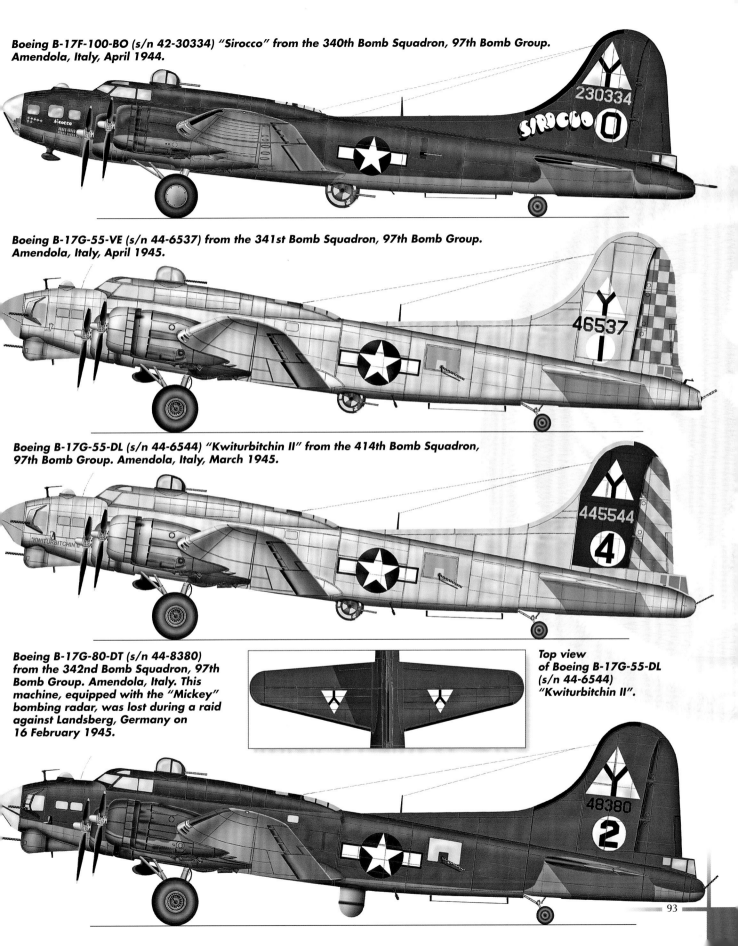

Boeing B-17F-100-BO (s/n 42-30334) "Sirocco" from the 340th Bomb Squadron, 97th Bomb Group. Amendola, Italy, April 1944.

Boeing B-17G-55-VE (s/n 44-6537) from the 341st Bomb Squadron, 97th Bomb Group. Amendola, Italy, April 1945.

Boeing B-17G-55-DL (s/n 44-6544) "Kwiturbitchin II" from the 414th Bomb Squadron, 97th Bomb Group. Amendola, Italy, March 1945.

Boeing B-17G-80-DT (s/n 44-8380) from the 342nd Bomb Squadron, 97th Bomb Group. Amendola, Italy. This machine, equipped with the "Mickey" bombing radar, was lost during a raid against Landsberg, Germany on 16 February 1945.

Top view of Boeing B-17G-55-DL (s/n 44-6544) "Kwiturbitchin II".

98TH BOMBARDMENT GROUP (HEAVY)

This group was made up at Barksdale Field (Louisiana) on 28 January 1942 and activated on the following 3 February with its B-24 Liberators. Subsequently, it did its training at Fort Myers and Drane Field also in Florida. The 98th left for the Middle East in an emergency on 15 July 1942 and reached Palestine at the end of July. Based at Ramat-David, it carried out its first mission against Mersa Matruh in Egypt on 1 August. The group was initially assigned to the USMEAF (United States Middle East Air Force) then was assigned to the 9th Air Force in November 1942. With its fleet of forty-one B-24s, it carried out the low-level raid against the Ploesti oil refineries in Rumania on 1 August 1943 (Operation Tidal Wave). The 98th was put under the command of the 12th Air Force in September and October 1943, and on 1 November of the same year, it joined the 15th Air Force after settling at Brindisi in Italy. It carried on fighting the Germans and finished the war at Lecce, still in Italy. It carried out 417 missions, being awarded 15 "Battle Streamers" as well as two Presidential Unit Citations. The group returned stateside in April-May 1945 and was renamed the 98th Bombardment Group (Very Heavy). It was finally disbanded on 10 November 1945.

The 98th Bombardment Group (Heavy) comprised the following squadrons

— **343rd Bomb Squadron (H)**
— **344th Bomb Squadron (H)**
— **345th Bomb Squadron (H)**
— **415th Bomb Squadron (H)**

For the tactical symbols see the profiles.

On his base at Manduria, Italy, Lieutenant Reuben Weltha, surrounded by his crew inscribing the number of missions carried out by his plane, B-24D-60 Liberator (s/n 41-11766) from the 345th BS (98th BG). Note the large number of missions and the countries "visited"...(USAF)

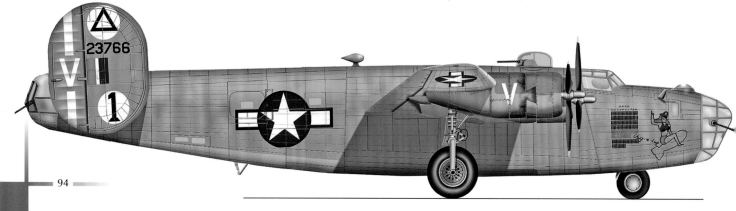

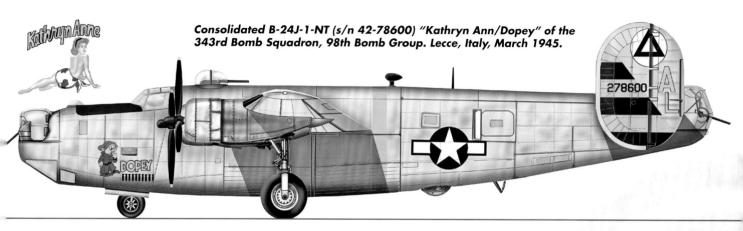

Consolidated B-24J-1-NT (s/n 42-78600) "Kathryn Ann/Dopey" of the 343rd Bomb Squadron, 98th Bomb Group. Lecce, Italy, March 1945.

99TH BOMBARDMENT GROUP (H)

In November 1943, the 99th Bombardment Group was assigned to the 15th Air Force and moved from Oudna, Tunisia to Tortorella, Italy a month later.

On 23 April 1944, with its B-17s the group bombed an aircraft factory situated at Wiener-Neustadt, Austria, going through very heavy flak and driving off very determined attacks by enemy fighters; despite this opposition the group didn't lose any planes and carried out its mission successfully. After being awarded a first DUC with the 12th Air Force, the 99th was awarded a second one for its action during this mission. It took part on 20 February in the "Big Week", the air raid campaign against the German aircraft industry.

The 99th BG went to the Soviet Union during a "shuttle" mission on 2 June 1944. In order to bomb a marshalling yard in Hungary, it landed in fact at Poltava, in the Ukraine, which it left four days later to carry out its bombing mission against a German airfield in Rumania. It returned to Poltava then to its base at Tortorella, bombing a German airfield in Rumania on the way.

B-17G-50 s/n 44-6372 from the 346th BS taking off from its Italian base in very tricky conditions due to the runway being completely soaked by the rains during the winter of 1944-45. The tail is painted red the squadron colour. (USAF)

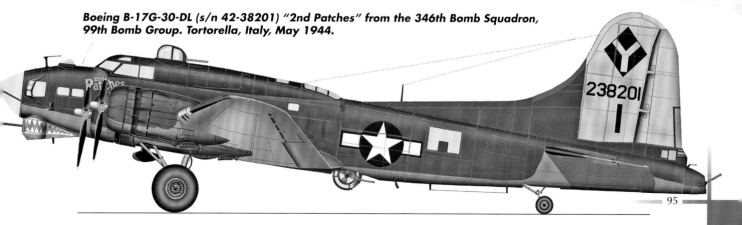

Boeing B-17G-30-DL (s/n 42-38201) "2nd Patches" from the 346th Bomb Squadron, 99th Bomb Group. Tortorella, Italy, May 1944.

The group bombed artillery positions and communication networks near Toulon in Southern France on 13 and 14 August and supported the landings in Provence directly on the 15th.

The 99th Bombardment Group (Heavy) which was disbanded on 8 November 1945 was made up of four squadrons:

- **346th Bomb Squadron** (**H**): Letter "Y" in a white lozenge (the 99th BG markings) and tactical code in Roman numerals "I", squadron distinctive colour: red.

- **347th Bomb Squadron** (**H**): Letter "Y" in a white lozenge (the 99th BG markings) and tactical code in Roman numerals "II", squadron distinctive colour: white.

- **348th Bomb Squadron** (**H**): Letter "Y" in a white lozenge (the 99th BG markings) and tactical code in Roman numerals "III", squadron distinctive colour: yellow.

- **416th Bomb Squadron** (**H**): Letter "Y" in a white lozenge (the 99th BG markings) and tactical code in Roman numerals "IV", squadron distinctive colour: Blue.

Some B-17Gs from the 348th BS (99th BG) returning home to base after a raid against a railway bridge at Szob (Hungary), on 20 September 1944. In the foreground is s/n 44-6385 (58 missions) and behind it is s/n 44-8164 "Section Eight". (USAF)

Boeing B-17G-50 DL (s/n 44-6430) from the 347th Bomb Squadron, 99th Bomb Group, Tortorella, Italy. This machine was shot down by flak over Yugoslavia on 7 November 1944, with all the crew managing to bail out.

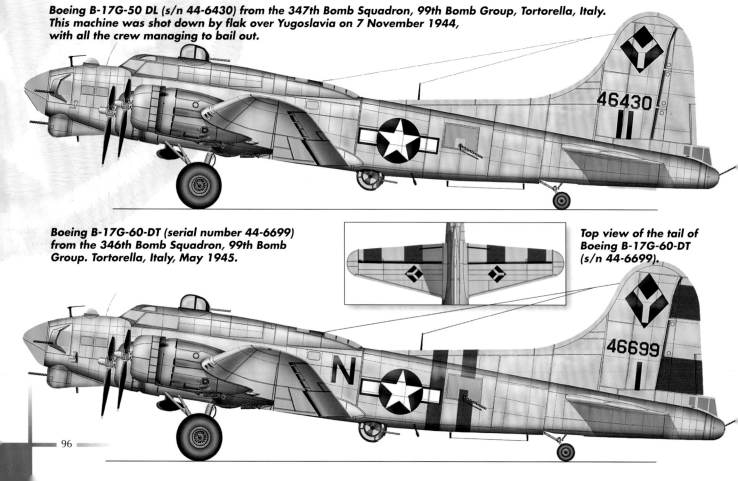

Boeing B-17G-60-DT (serial number 44-6699) from the 346th Bomb Squadron, 99th Bomb Group. Tortorella, Italy, May 1945.

Top view of the tail of Boeing B-17G-60-DT (s/n 44-6699).

WHO FEARS ?

301st Bombardment Group (Heavy)

It was transferred from the 12th to the 15th Air Force with its B-17s in November 1943 and moved to Cerignola in Italy the following month. It thereafter concentrated most of its attacks against the oil refineries, communications networks and industrial zones in Western and Central Europe.

In January 1944, the group carried out ground support missions for the troops in the Anzio and Monte Cassino areas in Italy.

After a first DUC awarded whilst in the 12th Air Force, the group was awarded a second one on 25 February 1944 for a mission carried out over Germany during which the group bombed the Regensburg aircraft assembly plants in spite of determined attacks by enemy fighters. The group continued its missions in Europe and in August 1944 took part in the Provence landings. In the Balkans the 301st destroyed targets to facilitate the advance of Soviet troops, and then supported the advance made by Allied troops in the north of Italy.

The group returned stateside in July 1945, was renamed 301st Bombardment Group (Very Heavy) and then was disbanded on 15 October 1945.

The 301st Bombardment Group (H) was made up of four squadrons:

— **32nd Bomb Squadron (H).** Marking of the 301st BG represented by a "Y" inside a square and the figure "1" on the tail. No distinctive colour.

— **352nd Bomb Squadron (H).** Marking of the 301st BG represented by a "Y" inside a square and the figure "2" on the tail. No distinctive colour. Insignia unknown.

— **353rd Bomb Squadron (H).** Marking of the 301st BG represented by a "Y" inside a square and the figure "3" on the tail. No distinctive colour. Insignia unknown.

— **419th Bomb Squadron (H).** Marking of the 301st BG represented by a "Y" inside a square and the figure "4" on the tail. No distinctive colour. Insignia unknown.

Above. **A box of Flying fortresses from the 353rd BS (301st BG) flying over the Alps during a raid on a marshalling yard in Vienna on 12 March 1945. In the foreground, B-17G-50-VE s/n 44-8105 equipped with an H2X "Mickey" radar. The sphere of the AN/APQ-13 aerial can be seen under the fuselage.** *(USAF)*

Boeing B-17F-50-DL (s/n 42-3343) "Slick Chick" from the 32nd Bomb Squadron, 301st Bomb Group, Lucera, Italy, January 1944. After the 15th Air Force was formed, the first B-17Fs from the 301st Bomb Group arriving in Italy did not yet bear the group's new markings. This B-17F finished the war with 75 missions to its credit.

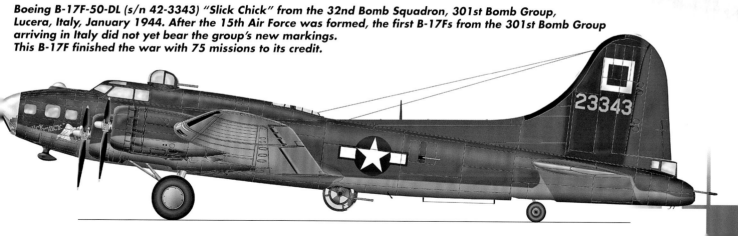

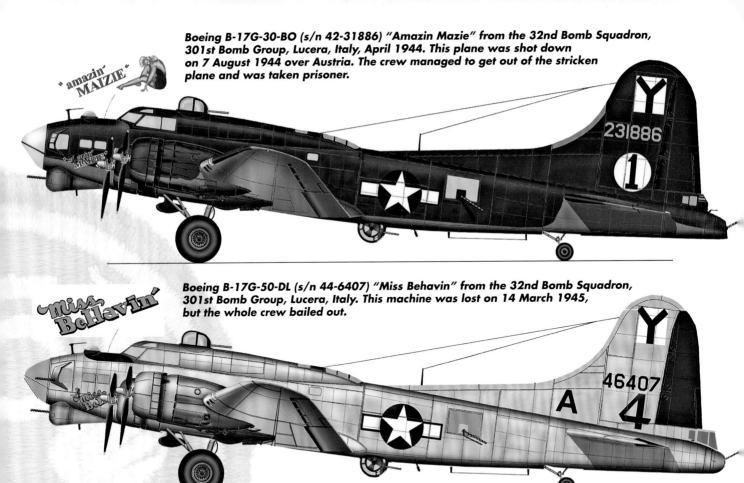

Boeing B-17G-30-BO (s/n 42-31886) "Amazin Mazie" from the 32nd Bomb Squadron, 301st Bomb Group, Lucera, Italy, April 1944. This plane was shot down on 7 August 1944 over Austria. The crew managed to get out of the stricken plane and was taken prisoner.

Boeing B-17G-50-DL (s/n 44-6407) "Miss Behavin" from the 32nd Bomb Squadron, 301st Bomb Group, Lucera, Italy. This machine was lost on 14 March 1945, but the whole crew bailed out.

376TH BOMBARDMENT GROUP (HEAVY)

After Pearl harbour, the HALPRO (*Halverson Provisional Detachment* after its CO, Colonel Harry A. Halverson) unit, made up of members of the 98th Bombardment Group (Heavy), was set up at the beginning of 1942. Given 23 consolidated B-24D Liberators, originally it was to have gone to China to be attached to the 10th Air Force to carry out raids on Tokyo. When it arrived in Palestine in October 1942, HALPRO learnt that its Chinese airfield had been overrun by Japanese troops. As at the same moment the Afrika Korps was getting ready to attack Allied forces in North Africa, the unit was quickly turned aside from its original mission and engaged in North Africa. Redesignated 376th Bombardment Group (H) and activated on 31 October 1942 on the base at Lydda, Palestine, it was initially assigned to the 9th Air Force. Shortly afterwards the HALPRO

personnel was transferred with its B-24s to the 376th Bombardment Group (H) and it was from airfields in Egypt that the "Liberandos" (their new nickname) carried out interdiction raids against shipping and North African ports. Based at Benghazi, Lybia, it took part in Operation Tidal Wave, the raid on the oil refineries at Ploesti, Rumania.

In September 1943, the 376th BG was assigned to the 12th Air Force for a short while, then in November 1943, it joined the 15th Air Force on its base at San Pancrazio, Italy from where it took part in the campaign against targets situated in Southern Europe and the Balkans.

During its four years of operations, the 376th BG carried out 451 missions, was awarded three DUCs and fifteen other citations, the "Liberandos" losing a total of 169 machines.

"Angie the Ox", B-24D-15-CO (s/n 41-24031) from the 515th BS (376th BG) flying over Sofia, the Bulgarian capital which the 15th AF had just bombed. (USAF)

The 376th Bombardment Group was made up of the following squadrons:
— 512th Bomb Squadron (H)
— 513th Bomb Squadron (H)
— 514th Bomb Squadron (H)
— 515th Bomb Squadron (H)
The group bore a distinctive marking after May 1944 (see profiles).

Consolidated B-24D-160-CO (s/n 42-72843) "Strawberry Bitch" from the 512th Bomb Squadron, 376th Bomb Group. San Pancrazio, Italy, December 1943.

Consolidated B-24H-10-CF (s/n 41-29279) from the 512th Bomb Squadron, 376th Bomb Group. San Pancrazio, Italy, February 1944.

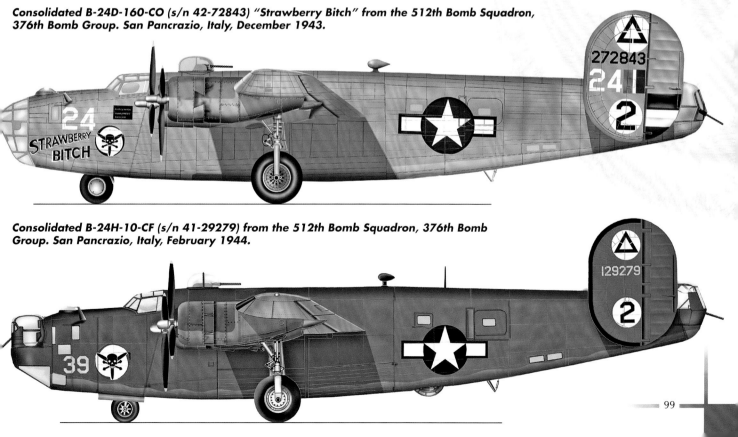

449TH BOMBARDMENT GROUP (HEAVY)

Sapientiam Ferimus

Activated on 1 May 1943 at Davis-Monthan, near Tuscon, Arizona it was originally part of the 47th Wing which comprised four heavy bombardment groups. The 449th, equipped with B-24 Liberators, ended its training in December 1943 and was assigned to the 15th Air Force on the airfield at Grottaglie in Italy. It reached its base by air, crossing by the South Atlantic route and flying over most of Africa to reach its destination in January 1944.

The 449th operated from this base from January 1944 to the end of the war in May 1945. it carried out 254 missions against targets situated in Central and Eastern Europe. The group returned stateside in May 1945.

It was made up of four squadrons:
— **716th Bomb Squadron (H)**
— **717th Bomb Squadron (H)**
— **718th Bomb Squadron (H)**
— **719th Bomb Squadron (H)**
(For the markings see the profiles).

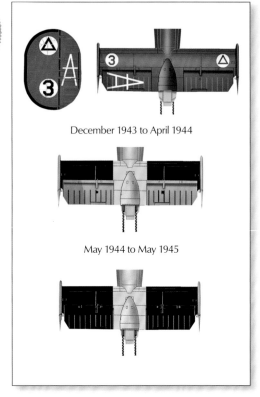

December 1943 to April 1944

May 1944 to May 1945

Consolidated B-24H-5-FO (s/n 42-52106) "Sunshine" from the 719th Bomb Squadron, 449th Bomb Group, Grottaglie, Italy, March 1944. This machine was recovered by the Luftwaffe after making a forced landing in enemy territory; its crew was taken prisoner.

Consolidated B-24H-15-FO (s/n 42-52434) "My Achin' Back" from the 718th Bomb Squadron, 449th Bomb Group, Grottaglie, Italy, January 1945.

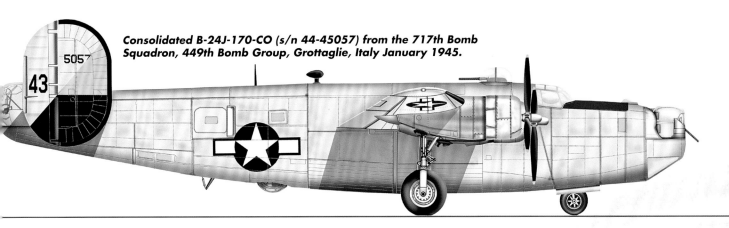

Consolidated B-24J-170-CO (s/n 44-45057) from the 717th Bomb Squadron, 449th Bomb Group, Grottaglie, Italy January 1945.

450TH BOMBARDMENT GROUP (HEAVY)

Made up on 6 April 1943, the 450th Bombardment Group (Heavy was activated on 1 May 1943). It was sent to Italy in December of the same year and based at Manduria with its B-24s, joining the 15th Air Force and starting operations against strategic targets in Western, Central Europe and the Balkans.

The group took part in the "Big Week" from 20 to 25 February 1944, by attacking the factories at Steyr in Austria and Regensburg in Germany. The 450th BG was awarded a DUC for having stood up to enemy fighter attacks and the flak in very bad weather conditions during the bombing of the Regensburg Messerschmitt factory on 25 February. It was awarded a second DUC for its mission on 5 April 1944 when it succeeded in getting through the swarms of enemy fighters to hit the marshalling yards at Ploesti. It also supported the landings in Provence and the advance of Soviet troops in the Balkans, then supported the Allied effort in Northern Italy. The group returned to the States in May 1945 and was disbanded on 15 October 1945.

The 450th Bombardment Group (H), nicknamed "Cottontails", was made up of four squadrons:
— 720th Bomb Squadron (H): tactical code from 1 to 20.
— 721st Bomb Squadron (H): tactical code from 21 to 39.
— 722nd Bomb Squadron (H): tactical code from 40 to 59.

— 723rd Bomb Squadron (H): tactical code from 60 to 99. For the group's markings see the profiles.

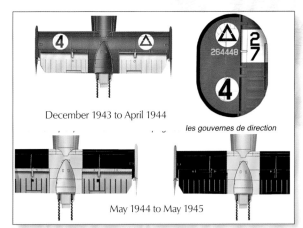

December 1943 to April 1944

les gouvernes de direction

May 1944 to May 1945

Above. **The left undercarriage leg of "Miss Fury", B-24-H-5-CF (s/n 41-29212) from the 721st BS (450th BG) broke on landing in the mud on the Manduria runway, as it was returning from a mission on 13 March 1944. Once repaired it was able to return to combat duty. (USAF)**

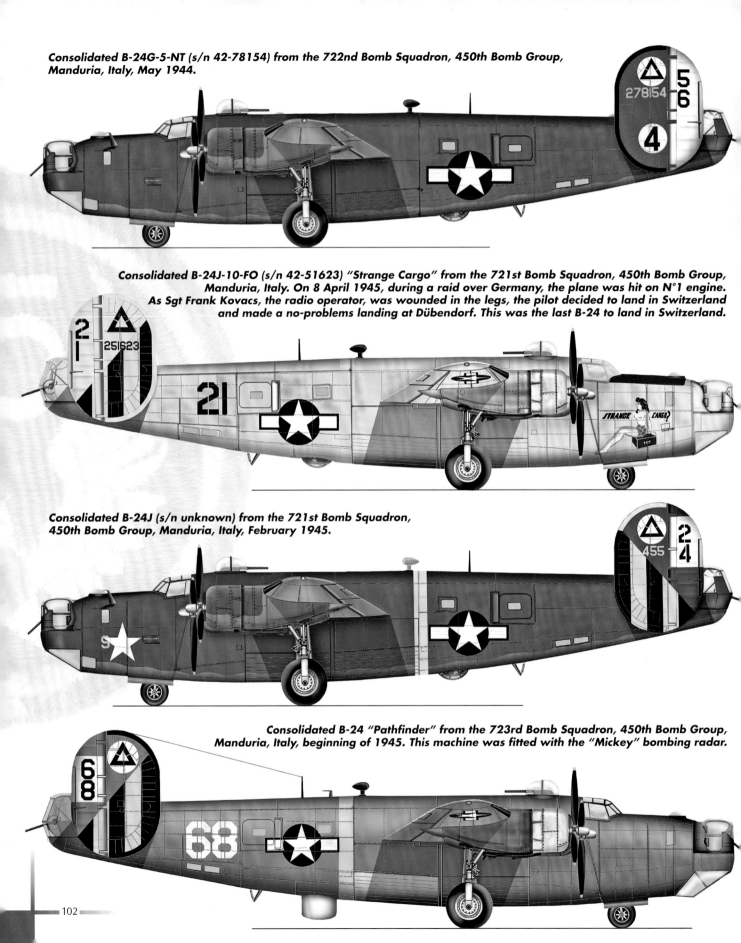

Consolidated B-24G-5-NT (s/n 42-78154) from the 722nd Bomb Squadron, 450th Bomb Group, Manduria, Italy, May 1944.

Consolidated B-24J-10-FO (s/n 42-51623) "Strange Cargo" from the 721st Bomb Squadron, 450th Bomb Group, Manduria, Italy. On 8 April 1945, during a raid over Germany, the plane was hit on N°1 engine. As Sgt Frank Kovacs, the radio operator, was wounded in the legs, the pilot decided to land in Switzerland and made a no-problems landing at Dübendorf. This was the last B-24 to land in Switzerland.

Consolidated B-24J (s/n unknown) from the 721st Bomb Squadron, 450th Bomb Group, Manduria, Italy, February 1945.

Consolidated B-24 "Pathfinder" from the 723rd Bomb Squadron, 450th Bomb Group, Manduria, Italy, beginning of 1945. This machine was fitted with the "Mickey" bombing radar.

451st Bombardment Group (Heavy)

Activated on 1 May 1943 at Davis Monthan, Arizona, the 451st Bombardment Group (Heavy) trained on B-24s before being sent to the Mediterranean front. It resumed its training in Algeria for a few weeks then joined the 15th Air Force and settled at the base at Gioia de Colle in Italy.

The group took part in strategic bombing missions over Europe. It was awarded a DUC for its conduct in three missions: the first against an aircraft factory at Regensburg, in Germany on 25 February 1944 during the "Big Week"; the second against the oil refineries and the marshalling yards at Ploesti in

Above. **View in flight over Italy in July 1944 of B-24H (s/n 41-29840) "Screamin Meemie II" from the 726th Bomb Squadron (451st Bomb Group). The markings on the tail are red.** *(USAF)*

sion. It contributed to preparing the way for the landings in Provence in August 1944, transported supplies for the troops stationed in Italy in September 1944 and also supported the Allied troops advancing in Northern Italy.

The group finished the war on the base at Castelluccio di Sauri, still in Italy then returned stateside in June 1945 and was disbanded on 26 September 1945.

The 451st Bombardment Group (H) was made up of four squadrons:

— **724th Bomb Squadron (H):** tactical code from 01 to 24, distinctive colour: yellow.

— **725th Bomb Squadron (H):** tactical code from 25 to 49, distinctive colour; green.

— **726th Bomb Squadron (H):** tactical code from 50 to 74, distinctive colour: red.

— **727th Bomb Squadron (H):** tactical code from 75 to 99, distinctive colour: white.

The upper part of the tail was painted red and the lower part had a red circle representing the group marking.

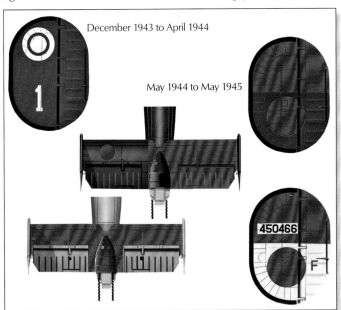

December 1943 to April 1944

May 1944 to May 1945

450466

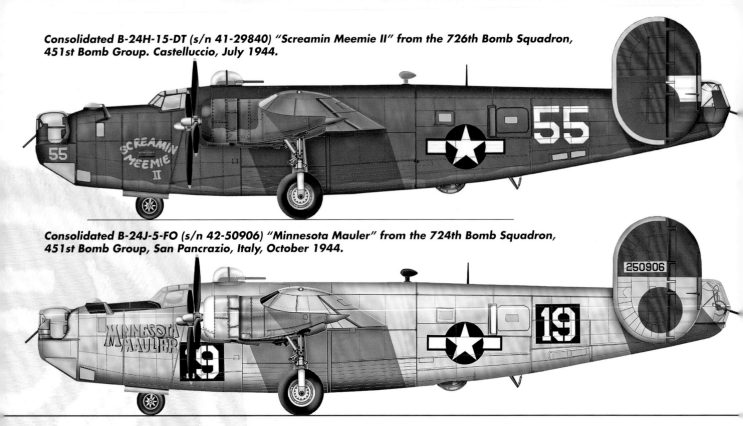

Consolidated B-24H-15-DT (s/n 41-29840) "Screamin Meemie II" from the 726th Bomb Squadron, 451st Bomb Group. Castelluccio, July 1944.

Consolidated B-24J-5-FO (s/n 42-50906) "Minnesota Mauler" from the 724th Bomb Squadron, 451st Bomb Group, San Pancrazio, Italy, October 1944.

454TH BOMBARDMENT GROUP (HEAVY)

Formed on 14 May 1943, the 454th Bombardment Group (Heavy) was activated on 1 June 1943 at Davis-Monthan. All the group's personnel gathered at McCook, Nebraska on 1 August and on 2 December 1943, the crews and the ground staff were sent to Mitchel field, New York, in order to get ready to deploy the group in North Africa using the South Atlantic route to reach Tunisia and do further training.

Assigned to the 15th Air Force, the group settled with its B-24s at San Giovanni in Italy from where it carried out 243 missions against more than 150 strategic targets in Western and Central Europe.

The 454th BG took part in the Allied advance on Rome, in the Provence landings and in the defeat of the Axis forces in Northern Italy. It was awarded a DUC after its missions against the "Hermann Göring" steelworks at Linz in Austria on 25 July 1944. The group was awarded a second Distinguished Unit Citation on 24 May 1945 for a similar action against, this time, the Bad Volsau Messerschmitt factory in Austria on 12 April 1945. After the Germans capitulated in May 1945, the 454th BG ended the war at San Giovanni and returned to the United States.

The 454th Bombardment Group (H) was made up of four squadrons:

- **736th Bomb Squadron (H)**: tactical code from 0 to 20, distinctive colour white.

- **737th Bomb Squadron (H)**: tactical code from 21 to 39, distinctive colour white.

- **738th Bomb Squadron (H)**: tactical code from 40 to 59, distinctive colour white.

- **739th Bomb Squadron (H)**: tactical code from 60 to 99, distinctive colour white.

For the group markings, see the profiles.

454th BG; December 1943 to April 1944

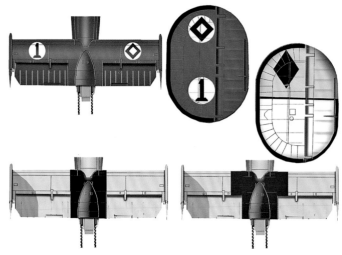

454th BG; May 1944 to May 1945

"*Fertile Mirtle*" *B-24G-16-NT from the 724th BS (451st BG) was lost in action over Austria on 23 September 1944. The tail markings are yellow.* (USAF)

Consolidated B-24H-10-CF (s/n 42-64459) "Slip Stream" (name on the right-hand side) from the 738th Bomb Squadron, 454th Bomb Group, San Giovanni, Italy, beginning of 1944.

Consolidated B-24M-5-FO (s/n 44-50582) from the 739th Bomb Squadron, 454th Bomb Group, San Giovanni, Italy, beginning of 1945.

455TH BOMBARDMENT GROUP (HEAVY)

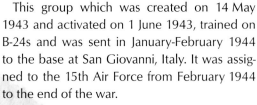

This group which was created on 14 May 1943 and activated on 1 June 1943, trained on B-24s and was sent in January-February 1944 to the base at San Giovanni, Italy. It was assigned to the 15th Air Force from February 1944 to the end of the war.

From the outset, it carried out bombing missions against strategic targets like factories, marshalling yards, oil refineries, storage areas, ports and aerodromes in Western, Central Europe and the Balkans. It also supported the ground troops at Anzio and Monte Cassino in March 1944.

The 455th was awarded Distinguished Unit citation for a mission carried out on 2 April 1944, during the 15th Air Force's campaign against enemy industry, by attacking the ball bearing factory at Steyr in Austria. It was awarded a second DUC for its action during the attack on 26 June 1944 against the oil refinery at Moosbierbaum, Austria despite very aggressive opposition from enemy fighters, a mission during which it lost several bombers. At the beginning of August 1944, it also took part in the Provence landings by bombing artillery positions.

Consolidated B-24H-10-FO (s/n 42-52267) from the 743rd Bomb Squadron, 455th Bomb Group, San Giovanni, Italy, beginning of 1944.

In April 1945, it supported the final Allied advance through Northern Italy, hitting bridges, artillery positions or troop concentrations. The 455th ended the war at San Giovanni and was disbanded in Italy in September 1945.

The 455th comprised four squadrons:
— **740th Bomb Squadron (H)**
— **741st Bomb Squadron (H)**
— **742nd Bomb Squadron (H)**
— **743rd Bomb Squadron (H)**

For the tactical codes and the distinctive colours, see the profiles.

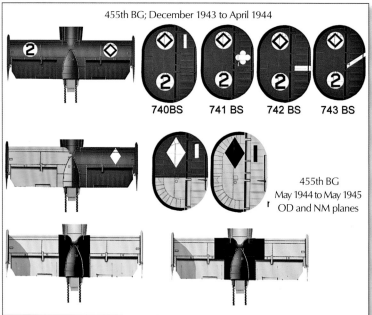

455th BG; December 1943 to April 1944

740BS   741 BS   742 BS   743 BS

455th BG
May 1944 to May 1945
OD and NM planes

Consolidated B-24H-10-FO (s/n 42-52267) of the 743rd Bomb Squadron, 455th Bomb Group. San Giovanni, Italy, beginning of 1944.

B-24s from the 455th BG leaving Bucharest, the capital of Rumania, which they've just bombed, 4 April 1944. *(USAF)*

Consolidated B-24J-200-CO (s/n 44-41199) " Yo-Yo" of the 741st Bomb Squadron, 455th Bomb Group. San Giovanni, Italy, 1944.

456TH BOMBARDMENT GROUP (HEAVY)

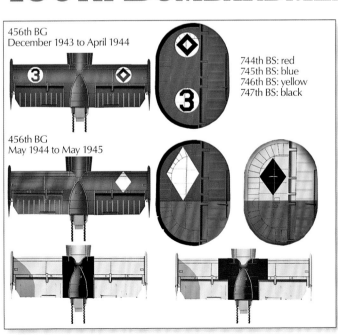

456th BG
December 1943 to April 1944

744th BS: red
745th BS: blue
746th BS: yellow
747th BS: black

456th BG
May 1944 to May 1945

The 456th Bombardment Group (Heavy) was activated at Wendover Field, Utah on 1 June 1943. After training on B-24; it left for Southern Europe in December 1943 and settled at Cerignola, Italy in January 1944, joining the 15th Air Force. Shortly afterwards it moved to Stornara near Foggia where it remained until the end of the war.

Its first operations took place in February 1944, when it attacked strategic targets in Austria, Italy and Rumania. It was awarded a DUC for its action on 10 May 1944 when, despite very bad weather conditions, it succeeded in bombing an industrial centre at Wiener-Neustadt, Austria, despite incessant enemy fighter opposition. In July and August 1944 it took part in preparing the landings in Provence. The group was awarded a second DUC for a mission carried out over Hungary on 2 July 1944, bombing the oil refineries at Budapest

in spite of severe enemy fighter attacks and very heavy anti-aircraft fire.

In April 1945, it supported the US Vth and the British VIIIth Armies during their advance in Northern Italy. It returned stateside in July 1945 and was disbanded on 17 October 1945.

The 456th Bombardment Group (H) was made up of four squadrons:

— **744th Bomb Squadron (H)**: tactical code represented by an individual red letter.

— **745th Bomb Squadron (H)**: tactical code represented by an individual blue letter.

— **746th Bomb Squadron (H)**: tactical code represented by an individual yellow letter.

— **747th Bomb Squadron (H)**: tactical code represented by an individual black letter.

For the group markings see the profiles.

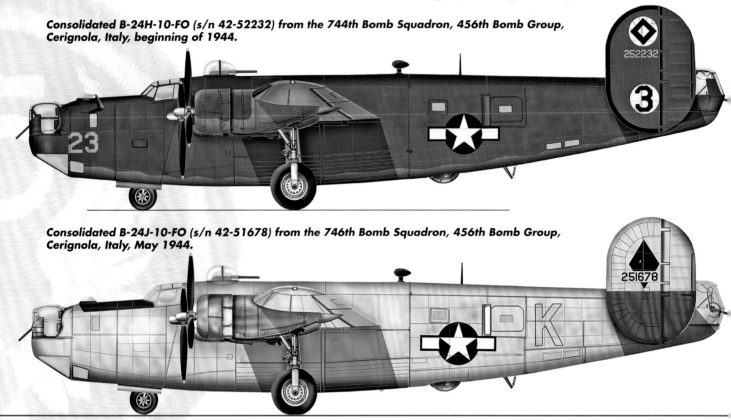

Consolidated B-24H-10-FO (s/n 42-52232) from the 744th Bomb Squadron, 456th Bomb Group, Cerignola, Italy, beginning of 1944.

Consolidated B-24J-10-FO (s/n 42-51678) from the 746th Bomb Squadron, 456th Bomb Group, Cerignola, Italy, May 1944.

459 TH BOMBARDMENT GROUP (HEAVY)

It was on the airfield at Alamogordo, New Mexico that this group was constituted on 19 May 1943 and activated on the following 1 July. It trained for combat on B-24s before being sent to the airfield at Giulia, Italy. Assigned to the 15th Air Force in January-February 1944, the 459th BG (H) was then engaged in strategic bombing from March 1944 to April 1945 in Western and Central Europe and the Balkans.

The group was awarded a DUC for having managed to get the 304th Wing through the enemy interceptor attacks and the very dense flak on 23 April 1944 during a raid on an airfield and an aircraft assembly plant at Bad Voslau, Austria. The group carried out other interdiction and support missions then in March 1944, it cut the enemy supply lines leading to the Anzio bridgehead, Italy. In August 1944, the group took

"Dogpatch Express", B-24-L10-FO (s/n 44-49750) from the 756th BS dropping its load of bombs on the railway lines near the town of Padua, Italy.
(USAF)

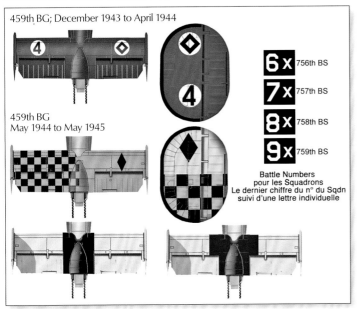

459th BG; December 1943 to April 1944

459th BG
May 1944 to May 1945

6 x	756th BS
7 x	757th BS
8 x	758th BS
9 x	759th BS

Battle Numbers
pour les Squadrons
Le dernier chiffre du n° du Sqdn
suivi d'une lettre individuelle

part in preparing for the landings in Provence (Operation Anvil) then supported the Allied ground troops in Northern Italy. The 459th BG ended the war at Guilia, Italy and then returned to the Sates where it was disbanded on 18 August 1945.

The 459th Bombardment Group (H) was made up of four squadrons:

— **756th Bomb Squadron (H)**: tactical code "6" followed by an individual letter, no distinctive colour.

– **757th Bomb Squadron (H)**: tactical code "7" followed by an individual letter, no distinctive colour.

— **758th Bomb Squadron (H)**: tactical code "8" followed by an individual letter, no distinctive colour.

— **759th Bomb Squadron (H)**: tactical code "9" followed by an individual letter, no distinctive colour.

For the group markings see the profiles.

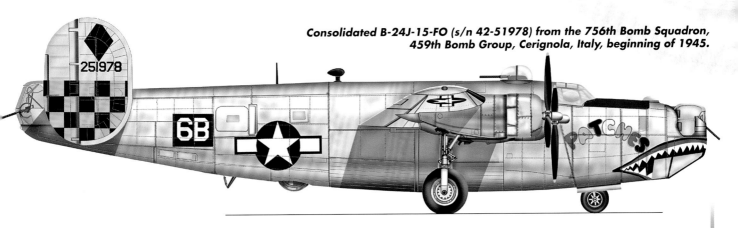

Consolidated B-24J-15-FO (s/n 42-51978) from the 756th Bomb Squadron, 459th Bomb Group, Cerignola, Italy, beginning of 1945.

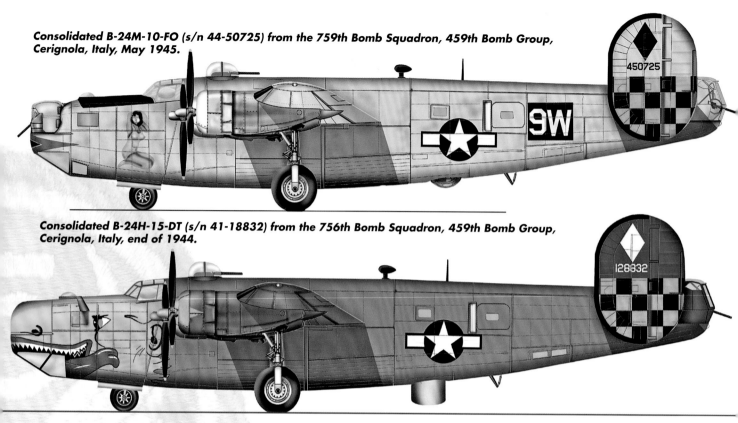

Consolidated B-24M-10-FO (s/n 44-50725) from the 759th Bomb Squadron, 459th Bomb Group, Cerignola, Italy, May 1945.

Consolidated B-24H-15-DT (s/n 41-18832) from the 756th Bomb Squadron, 459th Bomb Group, Cerignola, Italy, end of 1944.

460TH BOMBARDMENT GROUP (HEAVY)

The 460th Bombardment Group (Heavy) was created on w then activated on 1 July 1943 on the airfield at Alamogordo, New Mexico. After training it was sent to Italy with its B-24s, to the field at Spinazzola in February 1944 where it was incorporated into the 15th Air Force.

In March 1944, it carried out its first strategic raids in Western and Central Europe and in the Balkans. The group was awarded a DUC for having carried out a bombing raid in very bad weather under heavy fire from the enemy in order to destroy an aerodrome and aircraft installations at Zwolfaxing, Austria on 16 July 1944. It took part in August 1944 in the Provence landings, bombing the submarine shelters, marshalling yards and artillery positions in the assault zone. In order to facilitate the advance of Allied forces in Northern Italy, it then bombed bridges, viaducts, ammunitions depots, railway lines, etc.

The group ended the war at Spinazzola and in June 1945, it was sent to Trinidad, Cuba then to Brazil after having been assigned to Air Transport Command in order to repatriate personnel based in Europe back the States. The group was disbanded in Brazil on 26 September 1945.

The 460th Bombardment Group (H) was made up of four squadrons:

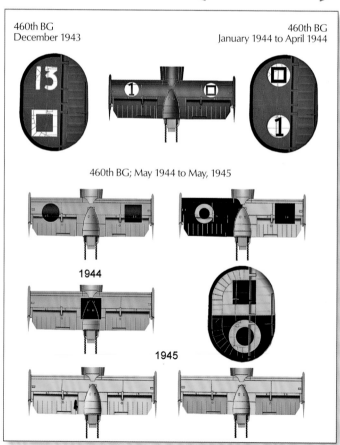

460th BG
December 1943

460th BG
January 1944 to April 1944

460th BG; May 1944 to May, 1945

1944

1945

Liberators from the 460th BG dropping fragmentation bombs over an aerodrome at Neuberg, Austria, on 26 March 1945.
(USAF)

— 760th Bomb Squadron (H)
— 761st Bomb Squadron (H)
— 762nd Bomb Squadron (H)
— 763rd Bomb Squadron (H).

Consolidated B-24H-15-DF (s/n 42-52337) "Cuddles" from the 763rd Bomb Squadron, 460th Bomb Group, Spinazzola, Italy, December 1943.

Consolidated B-24H-10-FO (s/n 41-29324) from the 460th Bomb Group. Spinazzola, Italy, February 1944.

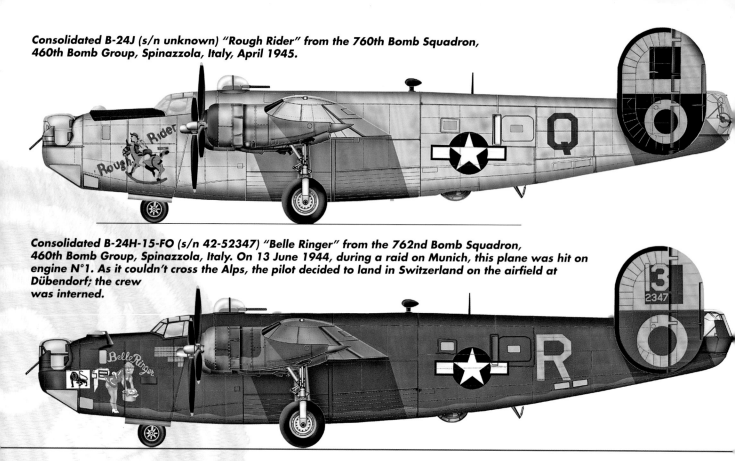

Consolidated B-24J (s/n unknown) "Rough Rider" from the 760th Bomb Squadron, 460th Bomb Group, Spinazzola, Italy, April 1945.

Consolidated B-24H-15-FO (s/n 42-52347) "Belle Ringer" from the 762nd Bomb Squadron, 460th Bomb Group, Spinazzola, Italy. On 13 June 1944, during a raid on Munich, this plane was hit on engine N°1. As it couldn't cross the Alps, the pilot decided to land in Switzerland on the airfield at Dübendorf; the crew was interned.

461ST BOMBARDMENT GROUP (HEAVY)

This heavy bomber group was formed on 19 May 1943 then activated the following 1 July at Wendover Field, Utah. It was sent to the Mediterranean front at the beginning of 1944, the air echelon crossing the South Atlantic with its B-24s and transiting by North Africa before reaching Torretto, Italy on 20 February 1944 when it was attached to the 15th Air Force.

It was in April 1944 that the 461st started its war missions, bombing lines of communications, factories and other strategic objectives in Western and Central Europe, and in the Balkans.

The group was awarded a DUC for a mission carried out on 13 April 1944 when it attacked a factory making aircraft parts in Budapest, Hungary after getting through heavy enemy defences. The 461st BG also carried out attacks against oil installations in France, in Poland Austria and Rumania. The group was awarded a second DUC after an air raid against the Ploesti oil refineries in Rumania in July 1944. In August 1944 it attacked artillery positions preparing for the Provence landings in

France. It supported the US 5th and the British 8th Armies' advance in Northern Italy in April 1945 and also took part in supplying prisoner of war camps in Austria in May 1945. The 461st finished the war at Torretto then returned to the States in July and was disbanded on 18 August 1945.

The 461st Bombardment Group was made up of four squadrons:
— **764th Bomb Squadron (H)**: tactical code from 1 to 19, distinctive colour yellow.
— **765th Bomb Squadron (H)**: tactical code from 20 to 39, distinctive colour white.
— **766th Bomb Squadron (H)**: tactical code from 40 to 59, distinctive colour green.
— **767th Bomb Squadron (H)**: tactical code from 60 to 79, distinctive colour red.

For the group markings see the profiles.

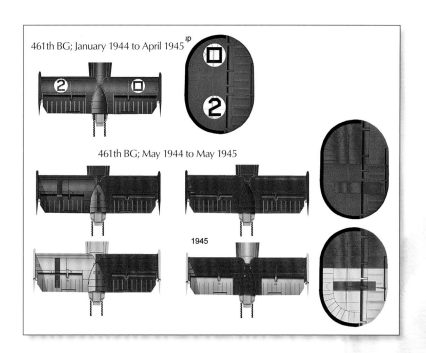

461th BG; January 1944 to April 1945 [ip]

461th BG; May 1944 to May 1945

1945

Consolidated B-24H-10-DT (s/n 41-28732) "Sweet Pea" from the 764th Bomb Squadron, 461st Bomb Group, Torretto, Italy. After a mission against Linz, Austria on 25 July 1944, this machine was riddled with bullets and crashed after attempting an emergency landing. The crew got out unhurt.

Consolidated B-24H-10-DT (s/n 41-28679) "Heaven can Wait" from the 766th Bomb Squadron, 461st Bomb Group, Torreto, Italy 1944.

Consolidated B-24H-15-DT (s/n 41-28913) from the 767th Bomb Squadron, 461st Bomb Group, Torreto, Italy. This machine was lost during a mission over Germany on 17 December 1944.

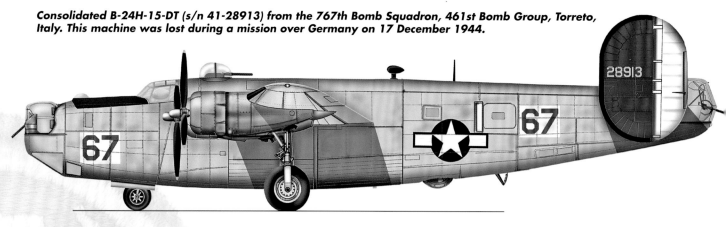

Consolidated B-24J-10-FO (s/n 42-51783) "What's Next" from the 765th Bomb Squadron, 461st Bomb Group, Torreto, Italy, beginning of 1945.

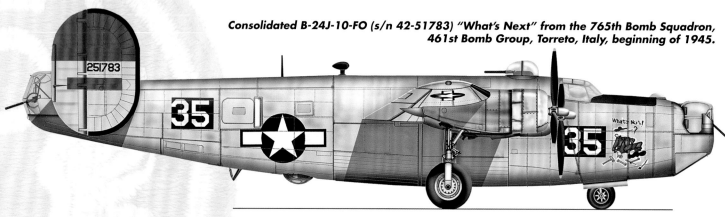

Consolidated B-24L-1-LO (s/n 44-49038) "Billie K" from the 765th Bomb Squadron, 461st Bomb Group. Torreto, Italy beginning of 1945. This plane was equipped with the "Mickey" radar system.

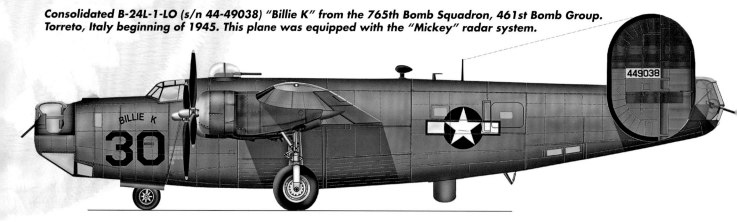

This Curtiss P-40F, belonging to Colonel Glantzberg, CO of the 461st Bomb Group, was used for liaison and as an assembly plane for the B-24 formations in the 461st BG.

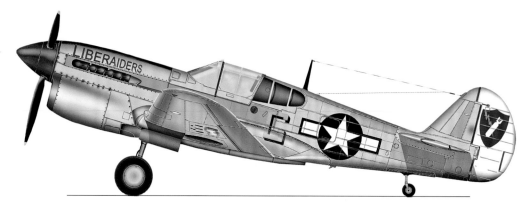

463RD BOMBARDMENT GROUP (HEAVY)

The 463rd Bombardment Group (Heavy) was made up on 19 May 1943 and activated on 1 August 1943; it was one of the last two B-17 units to train for duty on the European front. On 1 September 1943, it left Camp Rapid, Rapid City, South Dakota and carried on with its training in Florida before setting off over the South Atlantic to reach the airfield at Celone, near Foggia, Italy and being assigned to the 15th Air Force.

On 30 March 1944, the 463rd Bombardment group (H) carried out its first war mission, bombing an airfield at Imoski in Yugoslavia. It was awarded its first DUC after a mission carried out on 18 May 1944 when it bombed the oil refineries at Ploesti, Rumania. Because of the very bad weather conditions it didn't receive the message to abort the mission and carried on to its target running into very heavy opposition from enemy fighters and anti-aircraft defences. The group lost six planes but was saved by a large force of P-38s which came to the rescue and drove off the enemy fighters. In May 1944, the 463rd BG attacked enemy lines of communication during the campaign to free Rome then in August 1944 it took part in the landings in Provence.

It was in March 1945 that the 463rd was awarded its second DUC for a raid on the 24th against the Daimler-Benz armoured vehicles factory in Berlin. On 26 April 1945, the group carried out its 222nd and last combat mission. On top of its two DUCs, it was also awarded many other decorations. At the end of the war the 463rd with the 483rd BG, was part of a special detachment whose job was to transfer US 5th Army infantrymen from Naples to Casablanca before they returned to the States. The group ended the war at Celone then was disbanded on 15 September 1945.

The 463rd Bombardment Group (H) was made up of four squadrons:
— **772nd Bomb Squadron (H)**
— **773rd Bomb Squadron (H)**
— **774th Bomb Squadron (H)**
— **775th Bomb Squadron (H)**

All the group's squadrons bore a yellow distinctive colour (see profiles)

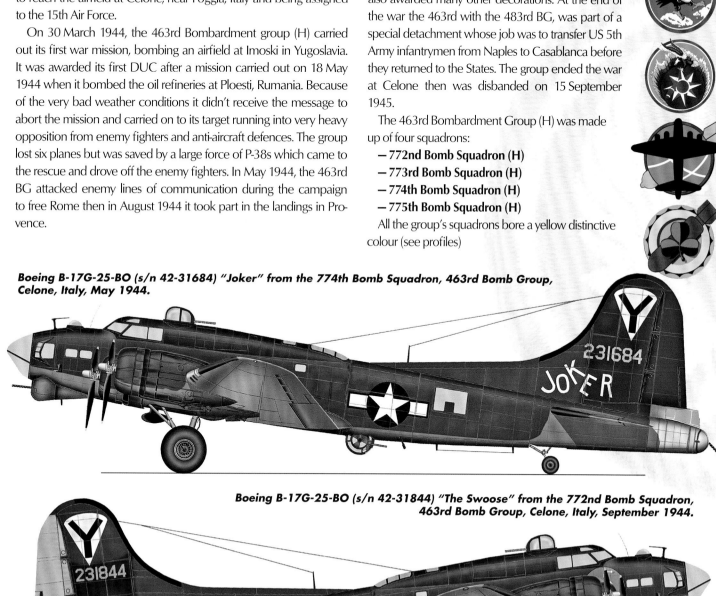

Boeing B-17G-25-BO (s/n 42-31684) "Joker" from the 774th Bomb Squadron, 463rd Bomb Group, Celone, Italy, May 1944.

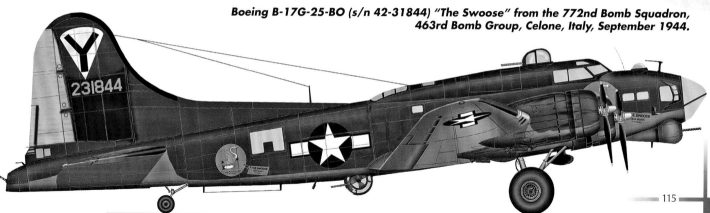

Boeing B-17G-25-BO (s/n 42-31844) "The Swoose" from the 772nd Bomb Squadron, 463rd Bomb Group, Celone, Italy, September 1944.

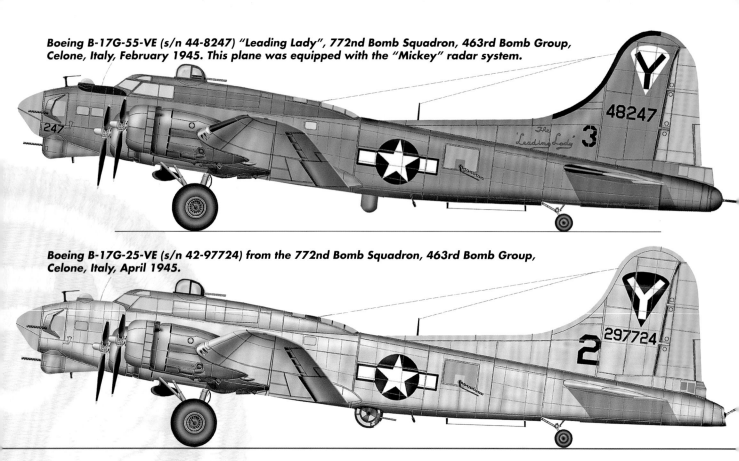

Boeing B-17G-55-VE (s/n 44-8247) "Leading Lady", 772nd Bomb Squadron, 463rd Bomb Group, Celone, Italy, February 1945. This plane was equipped with the "Mickey" radar system.

Boeing B-17G-25-VE (s/n 42-97724) from the 772nd Bomb Squadron, 463rd Bomb Group, Celone, Italy, April 1945.

464TH BOMBARDMENT GROUP (HEAVY)

Activated on 1 August 1943 at Wendover Field, Utah, the 464th Bombardment Group (Heavy), equipped with B-24s started training at Orlando, Florida the following month.

In order to reach Oudna in Tunisia on 9 March 1944, the crews used the South Atlantic route then after training again, settled on the base at Gioia del Cole, Italy on 21 April 1944. On the 30th, the group carried out its first combat mission against the marshalling yard at Castel Maggiore. On 2 May 1944, it carried out a new mission against the yard at Parma.

Installed on the base at Pantanella since 1 June 1944, the 464th BG (H) bombed Vienna but during the raid the B-24 belonging to the Group's CO was lost. The group ended the war on the field at Pantanella after having carrying out 210 combat sorties and losing 138 planes. It was disbanded in Trinidad, Cuba on 31 July 1945.

The 464th Bombardment Group (H) was made up of four squadrons:

— **776th Bomb Squadron (H)**: tactical code represented by a red individual letter of the squadron.

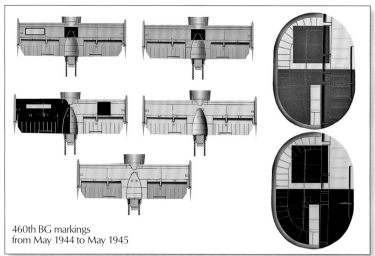

460th BG markings
from May 1944 to May 1945

— **777th Bomb Squadron (H)**: tactical code represented by a yellow individual letter of the squadron.

— **778th Bomb Squadron (H)**: tactical code represented by a white individual letter on a black square.

— **779th Bomb Squadron (H)**: tactical code represented by a black individual letter of the Squadron.

For the group markings see the profiles.

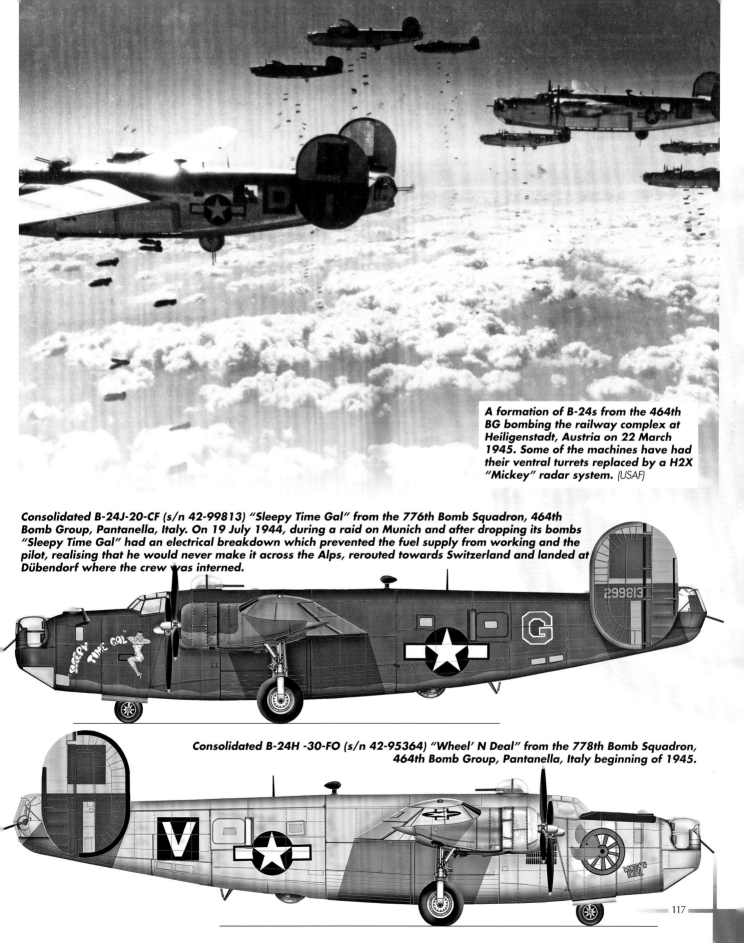

A formation of B-24s from the 464th BG bombing the railway complex at Heiligenstadt, Austria on 22 March 1945. Some of the machines have had their ventral turrets replaced by a H2X "Mickey" radar system. (USAF)

Consolidated B-24J-20-CF (s/n 42-99813) "Sleepy Time Gal" from the 776th Bomb Squadron, 464th Bomb Group, Pantanella, Italy. On 19 July 1944, during a raid on Munich and after dropping its bombs "Sleepy Time Gal" had an electrical breakdown which prevented the fuel supply from working and the pilot, realising that he would never make it across the Alps, rerouted towards Switzerland and landed at Dübendorf where the crew was interned.

Consolidated B-24H -30-FO (s/n 42-95364) "Wheel' N Deal" from the 778th Bomb Squadron, 464th Bomb Group, Pantanella, Italy beginning of 1945.

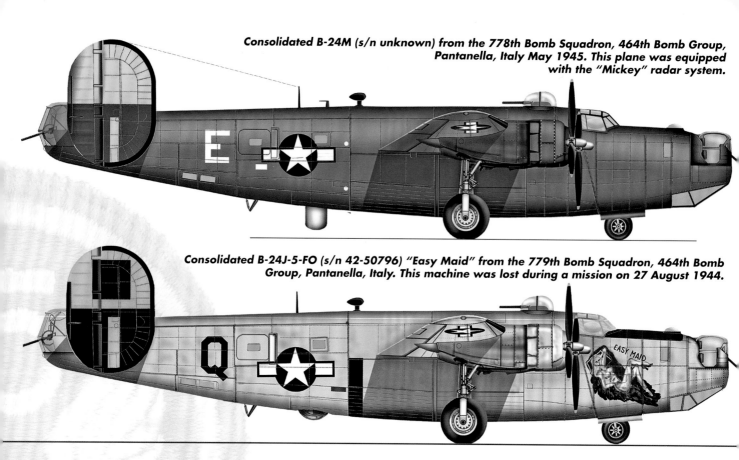

Consolidated B-24M (s/n unknown) from the 778th Bomb Squadron, 464th Bomb Group, Pantanella, Italy May 1945. This plane was equipped with the "Mickey" radar system.

Consolidated B-24J-5-FO (s/n 42-50796) "Easy Maid" from the 779th Bomb Squadron, 464th Bomb Group, Pantanella, Italy. This machine was lost during a mission on 27 August 1944.

465TH BOMBARDMENT GROUP (HEAVY)

It was at Alamogordo Army Airfield, New Mexico on 19 May 1943 that the 465th Bombardment Group (Heavy), was activated and equipped with B-24 Liberators. It then moved to Kerns, Utah for group training and personnel assignments. In February 1944, it was ordered to deploy on the Mediterranean front (MTO) which it reached by using the South Atlantic route before being assigned to the 15th Air Force. Based at Pantanella, Italy, in April 1944, it remained there until the end of the war.

The 465th BG operated as a strategic bomber unit until the end of April 1945 and during this period it attacked marshalling yards, port installations, oil refineries and their storage sites, aircraft factories as well a lot of other targets in Western and Central Europe and in the Balkans.

It was awarded a distinguished Unit Citation for bombing the marshalling yards and an oil refinery in Vienna on 8 July 1944 as well as

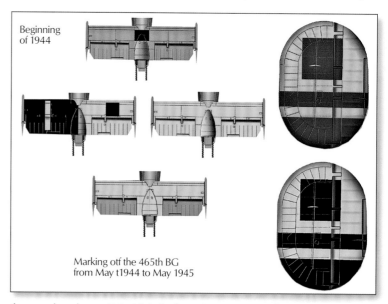

Beginning of 1944

Marking otf the 465th BG from May t1944 to May 1945

the steelworks at Friedrichshafen, Germany. In the same month it supported the landings in Provence and in October 1944 it supported the advance of Russian and Rumanian troops. In April 1945, it supported the Allied advance in Northern Italy.

Above. **This B-24J-200-CO (s/n 44-41159) from the 782nd BS (465th BG) is flying over the Sète region in France on 12 August 1944 preparing Operation Anvil, the Allied landing in Provence. This Liberator was shot down over Austria on 31 January 1945, and its crew taken prisoner after being able to bail out. Contrary to regulations, the only squadron marking is the white individual letter painted inside a disk at the rear of the fuselage.** (USAF)

After the armistice, the group was assigned to the "Green project" – repatriating troops who had remained stationed in the Mediterranean theatre, using the South Atlantic route, with extra seats being fitted in the B-24s to accommodate about 30 people. The 465th carried out this task until the end of July 1945 when it was disbanded.

The 465th Bombardment Group (H) was made up of four squadrons:

— **780th Bomb Squadron (H)**: tactical code in the form of a red individual letter of the squadron.

— **781st Bomb Squadron (H)**: tactical code in the form of a yellow individual letter of the squadron.

— **782nd Bomb Squadron (H)**: tactical code in the form of a white individual letter of the squadron.

— **783rd Bomb Squadron (H)**: tactical code in the form of a blue individual letter of the squadron.

Consolidated B-24H (s/n unknown) from the 780th Bomb Squadron from the 465th Bomb Group, Pantanella, Italy, beginning of 1945.

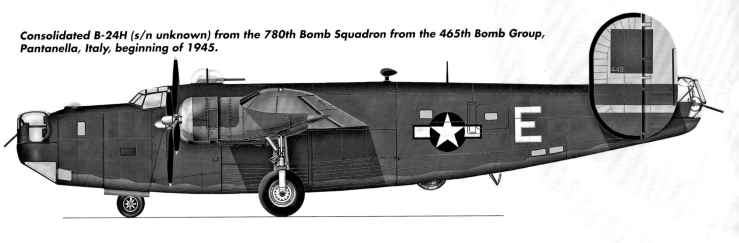

Consolidated B-24H (s/n unknown) from the 780th Bomb Squadron from the 465th Bomb Group, Pantanella, Italy, beginning of 1945.

Above. **Two Liberators from the 465th BG during a raid against the town of Ferrara, Italy. Note the differences in the markings depending on whether the planes are camouflaged or not. In the foreground "Memories" (B-24H-15-FO s/n 42-524xx) from the 782nd BS (white individual letter).**
(USAF)

Consolidated B-24H (s/n unknown) from the 781st Bomb Squadron from the 465th Bomb Group. Pantanella, Italy 1945.

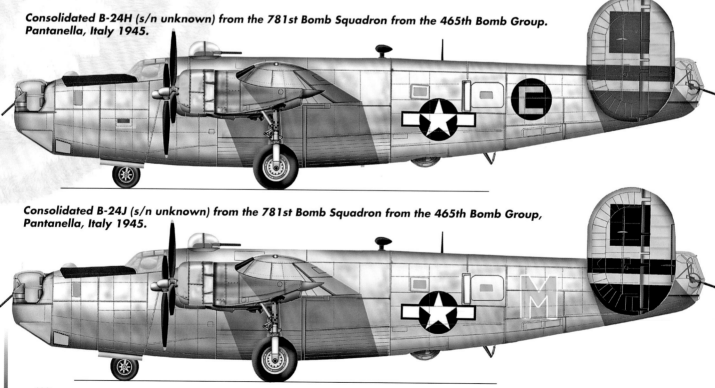

Consolidated B-24J (s/n unknown) from the 781st Bomb Squadron from the 465th Bomb Group, Pantanella, Italy 1945.

483RD BOMBARDMENT GROUP (HEAVY)

This group was constituted on 14 September 1943 and activated on the 20th at Fairmont, Nebraska. It was equipped with B-17s with which it trained. Sent to the Mediterranean front, it was assigned to the 15th Air Force and settled at Tortorella in the south of Italy on 30 March 1944, before moving to Sterparone in April where it remained until the end of the war.

It carried out strategic long distance bombing missions against industrial targets including oil refineries, oilfields as well as the production sites in Southern Germany, Austria, France, Italy and the Balkans.

The 483rd was awarded a DUC for its escort raid on 18 July 1944 during which it faced a great number of fighters over its target, an aerodrome and installations situated at Memmingen, Germany. It was awarded a second DUC for driving off the attacks of fighters and getting through the anti-aircraft fire on 24 March 1945 during an attack on armoured vehicle factories in Berlin.

It then took part in preparing the landings in Provence in August 1944 and supported the ground forces in Northern Italy during the Allied offensive in April 1945. It carried on strategic bombing operations until the Germans capitulated in May 1945.

After the armistice it was assigned to the "Green project" of Air Transport Command (ATC) and thus repatriated troops by stages from the airfield at Pisa in Italy to Morocco. Its B-17s were fitted with seats for this and were able to carry 25 passengers.

After carrying out 215 combat missions during which it lost 75 machines, the group was disbanded on 25 September 1945 whilst still based at Pisa, Italy.

The 483rd Bombardment Group (H) was made up of four squadrons which had neither tactical codes nor distinctive colour.

— **815th Bomb Squadron (H)**
— **816th Bomb Squadron (H)**
— **817th Bomb Squadron (H)**
— **818th Bomb Squadron (H)**

For the group markings see the profiles.

Above.
This B-17G-50-DL (s/n 44-6325) from the 816th BS seen here bombing the Vienne-Schwechart oil refineries on 7 February 1945 was shot down a few days later in the same area. *(USAF)*

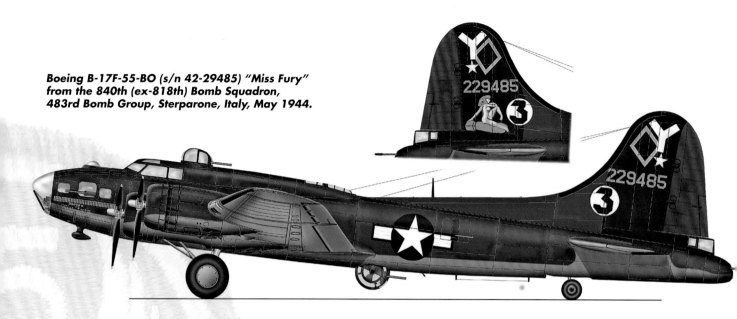

Boeing B-17F-55-BO (s/n 42-29485) "Miss Fury"
from the 840th (ex-818th) Bomb Squadron,
483rd Bomb Group, Sterparone, Italy, May 1944.

Boeing B-17G-35-BO (s/n 42-32044) "Good Deal" from the 815th Bomb Squadron,
483rd Bomb Group, Sterparone, Italy, May 1945.

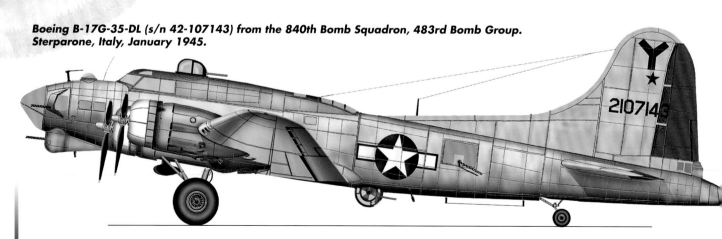

Boeing B-17G-35-DL (s/n 42-107143) from the 840th Bomb Squadron, 483rd Bomb Group.
Sterparone, Italy, January 1945.

484TH BOMBARDMENT GROUP (HEAVY)

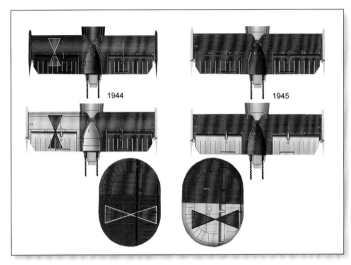

1944 1945

This group was created on 14 September 1943 and activated on the 20th of the same month at Harvard AAF, Nebraska after being equipped with B-24 Liberators. At the end of its training in February 1944 it was sent to the Mediterranean front. Assigned to the 15th Air Force, it settled at Torretto in the south of Italy.

It operated mainly as a strategic bomber unit from April 1944 to April 1945, attacking oil refineries and their storage sites, aircraft factories, heavy industry and communication links in Western, Central Europe and in the Balkans.

It was awarded its first DUC for bombing the Munich marshalling yards on 9 June 1944 in very difficult conditions. A second citation was awarded to it after a mission carried out without escort on 22 August 1944 during which it had to force its way through very violent enemy opposition in order to attack the oil storage installations in Vienna, Austria.

From April to June 1944, the 484th also took part in the advance on Rome, bombing bridges, supply depots, viaducts and marshalling yards. In September it carried fuel for the Allied ground forces in the South of France and in April 1945, it supported the final advance of the US 5th Army in the north of Italy. After the armistice, the 484th BG was assigned to the "Green Project" and repatriated troops stationed in Europe, using the South Atlantic route. It was fitted with 30 seats for this. This task lasted until the end of July 1945 when the unit was disbanded.

The 484th Bombardment Group (H) was made up of four squadrons:

— **824th Bomb Squadron (H)**: tactical code from 01 to 19, colour code uncertain – could be yellow, white, green or red.

— **825th Bomb Squadron (H)**: tactical code from 20 to 39, colour code uncertain – could be yellow, white, green or red.

— **826th Bomb Squadron (H)**: tactical code from 49 to 59, colour code uncertain – could be yellow, white, green or red.

— **827th Bomb Squadron (H)**: tactical code from 60 to 79, colour code uncertain – could be yellow, white, green or red.

For the group markings see the profiles.

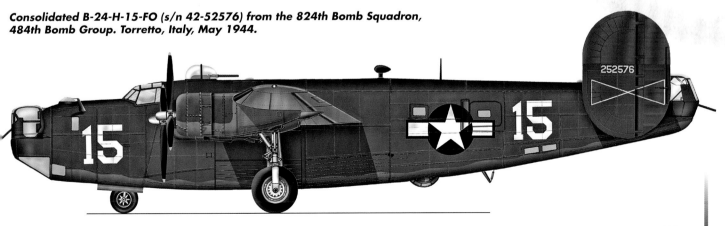

Consolidated B-24-H-15-FO (s/n 42-52576) from the 824th Bomb Squadron, 484th Bomb Group. Torretto, Italy, May 1944.

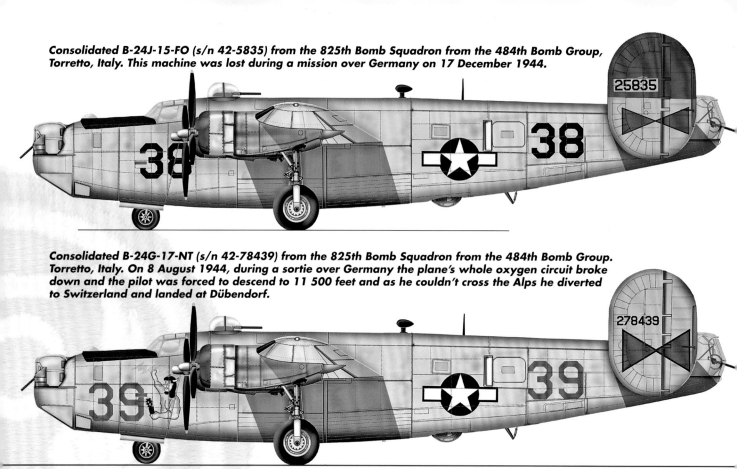

Consolidated B-24J-15-FO (s/n 42-5835) from the 825th Bomb Squadron from the 484th Bomb Group, Torretto, Italy. This machine was lost during a mission over Germany on 17 December 1944.

Consolidated B-24G-17-NT (s/n 42-78439) from the 825th Bomb Squadron from the 484th Bomb Group. Torretto, Italy. On 8 August 1944, during a sortie over Germany the plane's whole oxygen circuit broke down and the pilot was forced to descend to 11 500 feet and as he couldn't cross the Alps he diverted to Switzerland and landed at Dübendorf.

485TH BOMBARDMENT GROUP (HEAVY)

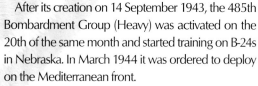

After its creation on 14 September 1943, the 485th Bombardment Group (Heavy) was activated on the 20th of the same month and started training on B-24s in Nebraska. In March 1944 it was ordered to deploy on the Mediterranean front.

The group was assigned to the 15th Air force and based at Venosa, in Southern Italy where it remained until the end of the war. It started its operations in May 1944. It carried out long distance strategic bombing operations against industrial targets situated in Western and Central Europe and the Balkans, bombing marshalling yards, oil refineries, aerodromes, heavy industry factory and other strategic targets. It was awarded a DUC for facing a very violent onslaught by enemy fighters while attacking an oil refinery at Vienna, Austria on 26 June 1944.

The 485th BG also carried out support and interdiction missions. It bombed ports, bridges, troop concentrations in August 1944 during the preparation for the Provence landings (Operation Anvil). In order to support the advance of the British 8th Army in Northern Italy, the group cut lines of communication and attacked other targets in March and April 1945. It returned to the United States in May 1945.

The 485th Bombardment Group (H) was made up of four squadrons:

— **828th Bomb Squadron (H)**: no tactical code, red distinctive colour sometimes on the front of the engine cowlings

— **829th Bomb Squadron (H)**: no tactical code, yellow distinctive colour sometimes on the front of the engine cowlings

— **830th Bomb Squadron (H)**: no tactical code, white distinctive colour sometimes on the front of the engine cowlings

— **831st Bomb Squadron (H)**: no tactical code, blue distinctive colour sometimes on the front of the engine cowlings

Opposite.
A Consolidated B-24H from the 485th Bomb Group flying over Bologna, part of which is blazing during the biggest bombing campaign carried out by the Mediterranean Air Force on 15 and 16 April 1944.
(USAF)

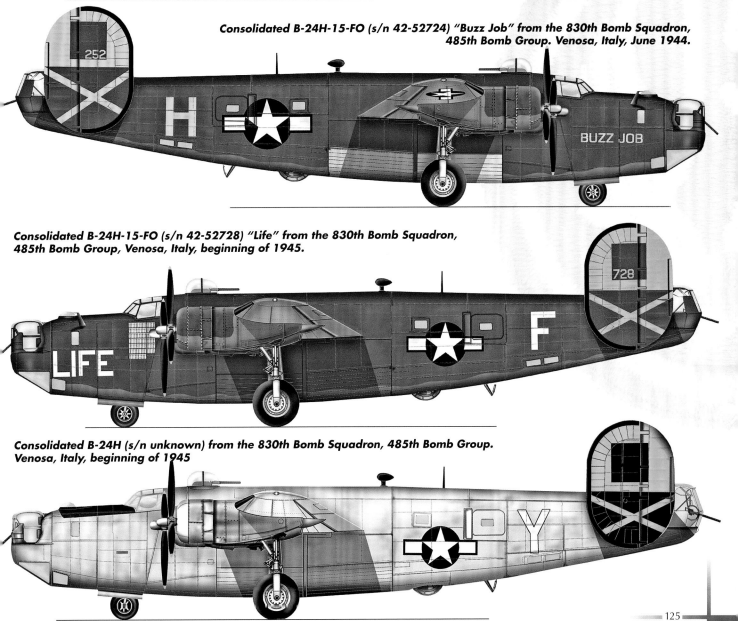

Consolidated B-24H-15-FO (s/n 42-52724) "Buzz Job" from the 830th Bomb Squadron, 485th Bomb Group. Venosa, Italy, June 1944.

Consolidated B-24H-15-FO (s/n 42-52728) "Life" from the 830th Bomb Squadron, 485th Bomb Group, Venosa, Italy, beginning of 1945.

Consolidated B-24H (s/n unknown) from the 830th Bomb Squadron, 485th Bomb Group. Venosa, Italy, beginning of 1945

859th Bomb Squadron (Heavy) (Special)

It was on 11 December 1944 that the 859th Bomb Squadron (Heavy) (Special), equipped with B-24s, was detached from the 8th Air Force to be incorporated into the 15th Air Force operating on the Mediterranean front (MTO). It was based at Brindisi, in Southern Italy from 17 December 1944. it carried out special operations in Western Europe, supporting the Normandy landings then supplying the resistance in Italy and in the Balkans.

It was at Brindisi on 20 January that the 859th BS joined the 885th BS to form the 15th Special Group.

885th Bomb Squadron (H) (S)

This squadron was equipped with B-24s and was part of the 15th Air Force in June 1944 and carried out special operations. It was assigned to the 15th Special Group in July 1944. As soon as it was joined by the 859th in January 1945 at Brindisi it formed the 15th Special Group.

Consolidated (Ford) B-24J-1-FO (s/n 42-50603) of the 859th BS (H) (S) from the 492nd BG. This plane was lost on 16 September 1944.

Les groupes de reconnaissance de la 15th AF

5th PRG (Photo Reconnaissance Group)

Lockheed F-5A (s/n unknown) of the 5th PRG.

In October 1944, the 5th PRG was transferred from the 12th to the 15th Air Force and settled on the base at Bari, Italy where it remained until October 1945 when it returned to Camp Kilmer, New Jersey.

The 5th Photo Reconnaissance Group was made up of three squadrons:

— **15th Photo Reconnaissance Squadron**: no tactical code and no distinctive colour.

— **32nd Photo Reconnaissance Squadron**: no tactical code and no distinctive colour.

— **37th Photo Reconnaissance Squadron**: no tactical code and no distinctive colour.

Opposite.
Lockheed F-4 from the 3rd PRG over the Tyrrhenian coast of Italy at the beginning of 1943.
(USAF)

154TH WEATHER RECONNAISSANCE SQUADRON (M)

This squadron dated back to the Great War and had had several designations, was renamed the 154th Weather Reconnaissance Squadron (Medium) on 12 May 1944.

Assigned to the 12th Air Force it left the United States in September 1942 and was based at Wattisham, Great Britain in the following October. From there it set off for Algeria in order to take part in Operation Torch, the landings in North Africa, settling at Oran on 9 November. The squadron was based on several airfields in Algeria and Morocco then took part in the Tunisian Campaign and finished this while it was based on the Korba airfield. It remained assigned to the 12th Air Force until January 1944 when it was transferred to the 15th Air Force. Based at Oran in Algeria, it carried out weather recce missions with its P-38/F-5 Lightnings. During the air raids made by the 15th Air Force's heavy bombers, the 154th WRS's role was to precede the formations and give them up-to-date weather information which they encountered on their way to the targets and on the return leg to base.

The squadron carried out 1 495 missions during the war and ended it on the base at Bari, Italy where it was stationed from February to July 1945. The 154th WRS was awarded a DUC for its actions on 17, 18 and 19 August 1944 over Rumania.

Tactical code from 01 to 20, horizontal white stripe on the tail fin for the planes camouflaged in olive drab and black for the bare metal planes.

Lockheed P-38J-15-LO Lightning (s/n 43-28744) from the 154th WRS.

15TH AIR FORCE FIGHTER GROUPS

1ST FIGHTER GROUP

Above. **A nice line-up of four Mustangs from the main squadrons in the 15th Air Force equipped with this fighter, flying over the Alps. From front to rear the P-51D belonging to the CO of the 317th Fighter Squadron (325th FG), the famous "Checkertail Clan", then an aircraft from the 302nd FS (332nd FG), followed by "Queen Marjorie" from the 4th FS (52nd FG) and finally at the rear a fighter from the 308th FS (31st FG).** (USAF)

It was in November 1943 while it was based at Cagliari in Sardinia that the 1st Fighter Group was transferred from the 12th to the 15th Air Force. It carried out bomber escort missions attacking targets in Western and Central Europe and in the Balkans. Stationed at Foggia, Italy, it took part in the landing at Anzio in January 1944, then in Provence in August of the same year; after two Distinguished Unit Citations awarded while serving in the 12th Air Force, it was awarded a third for protecting B-17s returning from bombing the Ploesti oil refineries in Rumania on 18 May 1944.

After moving to Lesina in March 1945, the 1st Fighter Group was stepped down on 16 October 1945 while still based in Italy.

The 1st Fighter Group was made up of three squadrons:

— **27th Fighter Squadron**: tactical code 1 to 30, red distinctive colour.

— **71st Fighter Squadron**: tactical code 31 to 59, black distinctive colour.

— **94th Fighter Squadron**: tactical code 60 to 90, yellow distinctive colour.

Lockheed P-38G-10 (s/n 42-13480) "Billie Jo". Pilot: Lt Donald D. Kienholz. 94th Fighter Squadron, 1st Fighter Group, Foggia, Italy, January 1944.

Opposite.
Mechanics from the 94th FS (1st FG) posing in front of P-38 Lightning "88" on an Italian airfield.
(USAF)

Lockheed P-38J (s/n unknown) "Old Rusty". Pilot: Lt Warren G. Campbell, 94th Fighter Squadron, 1st Fighter Group, Foggia, Italy, May 1944.

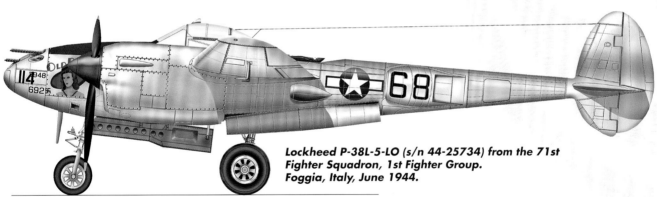

Lockheed P-38L-5-LO (s/n 44-25734) from the 71st Fighter Squadron, 1st Fighter Group. Foggia, Italy, June 1944.

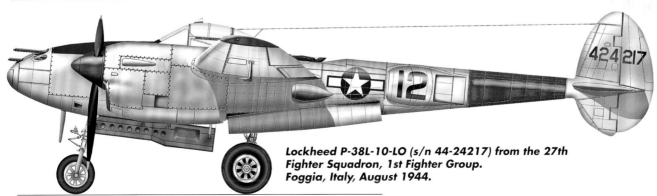

Lockheed P-38L-10-LO (s/n 44-24217) from the 27th Fighter Squadron, 1st Fighter Group. Foggia, Italy, August 1944.

14TH FIGHTER GROUP

This group was transferred from the 12th to the 15th Air Force in November 1943 while it was still based at Sainte-Marie-du-Zit, in Tunisia. In December, it moved to Triolo in Italy. It escorted 15th Air Force bombers attacking targets in Western and Central Europe and even escorted 12th Air Force bombers. On 2 April 1944 it was awarded a Distinguished Unit Citation for escorting bombers attacking a ball-bearing factory and an aircraft assembly plant at Steyr, Austria. At the end of July and beginning of August, the 14th carried out several "shuttle" missions between Russia and Italy then returned to its Italian base after spending three days on a Soviet base in Ukraine. Escorted by P-51 fighters during these missions, the 14th Fighter Group shot down thirty enemy aircraft and destroyed twelve others on the ground. The last shuttle mission by P-38 Lightnings was carried out by the group at the beginning of August 1944.

The 14th FG also carried out reconnaissance escort missions, supported the landings in Provence in August 1944 and on several occasions carried out ground attack missions over an area ranging from France to the Balkans. The 14th Fighter Group was deactivated in Italy in September 1945.

The 14th Fighter Group was made up of three squadrons:
— **48th Fighter Squadron**: tactical code from 1 to 30, distinctive colour: white.
— **49th Fighter Squadron**: tactical code from 31 to 60, distinctive colour: blue.
— **37th Fighter Squadron**: tactical code from 61 to 90, distinctive colour: red.

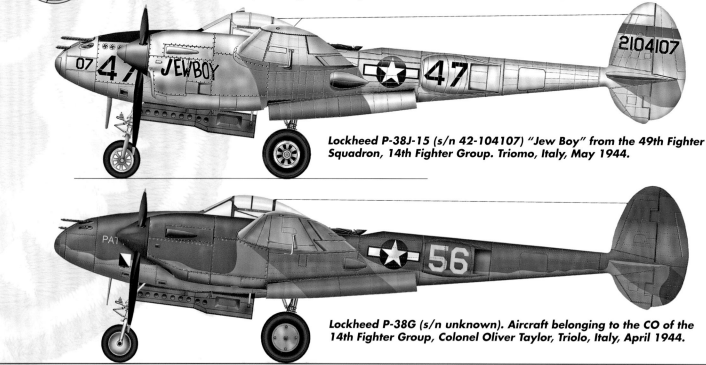

Lockheed P-38J-15 (s/n 42-104107) "Jew Boy" from the 49th Fighter Squadron, 14th Fighter Group. Triomo, Italy, May 1944.

Lockheed P-38G (s/n unknown). Aircraft belonging to the CO of the 14th Fighter Group, Colonel Oliver Taylor, Triolo, Italy, April 1944.

31ST FIGHTER GROUP

It was on the base at San Severo in Italy in April 1944 that the 31st Fighter Group was transferred from the 12th to the 15th Air Force and changed at the same time from flying Spitfires to P-51 Mustangs with which it carried out escort missions.

It was awarded a DUC on 21 April 1944 for carrying out a mission in very bad weather conditions while escorting bombers from the 15th AF in a raid on industrial targets in Rumania.

On several occasions, it escorted heavy bombers sent against targets in Continental Europe. It also escorted reconnaissance planes as well as C-47s engaged in parachute operations during the Provence

RETURN WITH HONOR

Opposite.
Four P-51D Mustangs from the 308th FS of the 31st FG posing for the camera: in the foreground "Smokey" (s/n 44-13974) flown by Captain Bill Smith, just behind it is "OKaye" (s/n 44-3311) belonging to Captain Leland P. "Tommy" Molland, an ace with 11 kills.
(USAF)

landings in August 1944. It also took part in operations in which the 15th Air Force attacked targets in Rumania on 22 July 1944, carrying out on this occasion a five-day shuttle mission to the USSR.

It was awarded a DUC for its action on 25 July when it escorted P-38s leaving Russia to carry out a raid on an aerodrome in Poland; the 31st FG attacked a convoy of German trucks and a group of fighter bombers before returning to its base at San Severo the following day.

When the Allies were engaged in their final offensive in the Northern Italy, the group was given ground attack missions against railways and main roads.

In March 1945, the 31st FG was stationed at Mondolfo, still in Italy then returned stateside in August where it was deactivated on the following 7 November.

The 31st Fighter Group was made up of three squadrons:
— **307th Fighter Squadron**: tactical code "MX", no distinctive colour.
— **308th Fighter Squadron**: tactical code "HL", no distinctive colour.
— **309th Fighter Squadron**: tactical code "WZ", no distinctive colour.

North American P-51B from the 308th Fighter Squadron, 31st Fighter Group. Castel Volturno, Italy, January 1944.

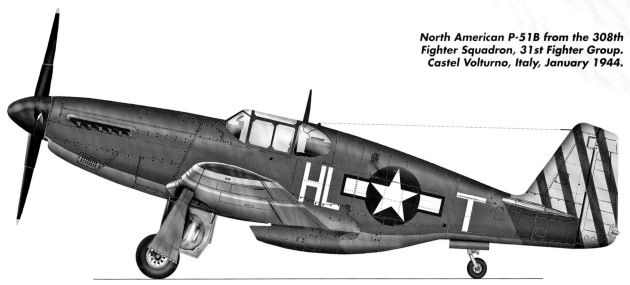

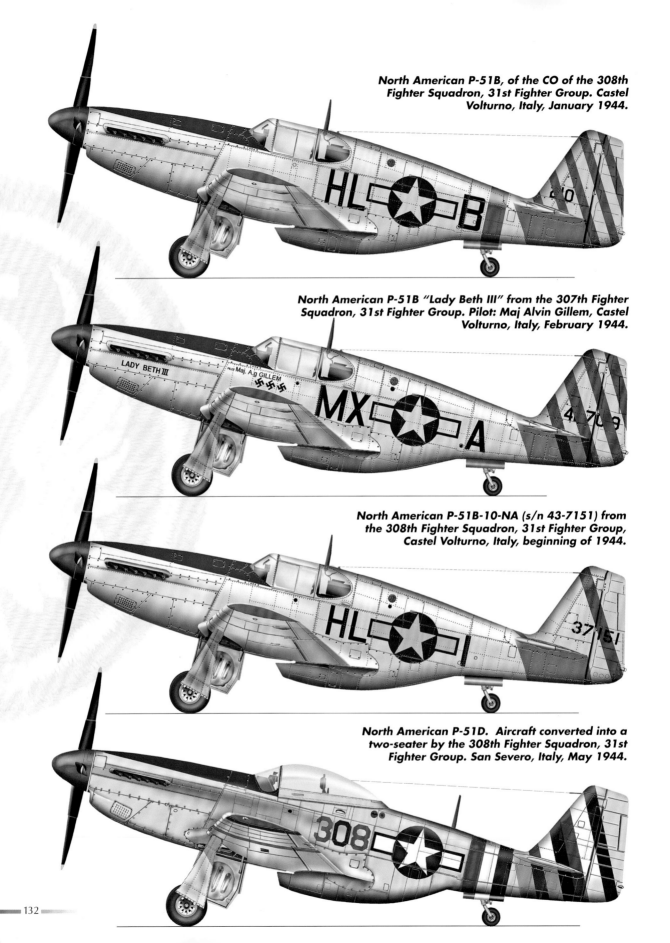

North American P-51B, of the CO of the 308th Fighter Squadron, 31st Fighter Group. Castel Volturno, Italy, January 1944.

North American P-51B "Lady Beth III" from the 307th Fighter Squadron, 31st Fighter Group. Pilot: Maj Alvin Gillem, Castel Volturno, Italy, February 1944.

North American P-51B-10-NA (s/n 43-7151) from the 308th Fighter Squadron, 31st Fighter Group, Castel Volturno, Italy, beginning of 1944.

North American P-51D. Aircraft converted into a two-seater by the 308th Fighter Squadron, 31st Fighter Group. San Severo, Italy, May 1944.

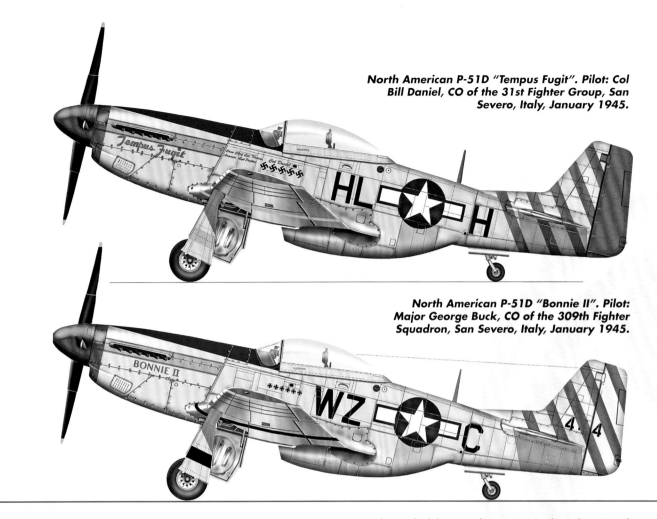

North American P-51D "Tempus Fugit". Pilot: Col Bill Daniel, CO of the 31st Fighter Group, San Severo, Italy, January 1945.

North American P-51D "Bonnie II". Pilot: Major George Buck, CO of the 309th Fighter Squadron, San Severo, Italy, January 1945.

52ND FIGHTER GROUP

It was assigned at first to the 12th Air Force and equipped with Spitfires, then in March 1944 it was transferred to the 15th AF and equipped with P-51s; whilst still based in Corsica, the group took part in combat operations on the Mediterranean front until the end of the war.

Based at Madna, Italy, the 52nd FG received its P-51s in April and May 1944 and its task was mainly escorting bombers raiding targets in Europe. It was awarded a DUC for a mission carried out on 9 June 1944, protecting bombers attacking aircraft factories, communications centres and supply routes situated in Germany. As well as escorting bombers from the 15th Air Force, the group also carried out ground support missions against important targets in Italy, France, Central Europe and the Balkans. It was awarded a second DUC for a raid against an airfield in Rumania on 31 August 1944 during which the group destroyed a large number of German and Rumanian fighters and transport planes.

At the end of the war, the group was based at Piagiolino, still in Italy. The 52nd Fighter Group returned to the United States in August 1945 and was disbanded on 7 November 1945.

The 52nd Fighter Group was made up of three squadrons:
— **2nd Fighter Squadron**: tactical code "QP", no distinctive colour.
— **4th Fighter Squadron**: tactical code "WD", no distinctive colour.
— **5th Fighter Squadron**: tactical code "VF", no distinctive colour.

Near a P-51, in July 1944, while inspecting Groups from the 15th AF, Lt.- General B.M. Giles, Chief of Staff of the USAAF talks to the 52nd FG's CO, Colonel Robert Levine. (USAF)

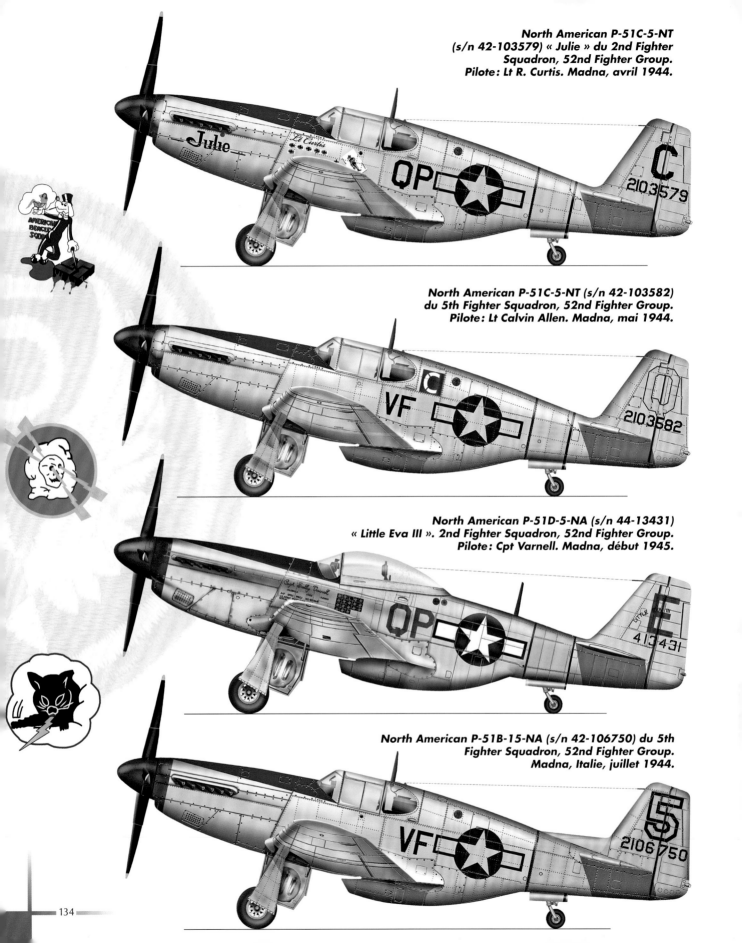

North American P-51C-5-NT
(s/n 42-103579) « Julie » du 2nd Fighter
Squadron, 52nd Fighter Group.
Pilote: Lt R. Curtis. Madna, avril 1944.

North American P-51C-5-NT (s/n 42-103582)
du 5th Fighter Squadron, 52nd Fighter Group.
Pilote: Lt Calvin Allen. Madna, mai 1944.

North American P-51D-5-NA (s/n 44-13431)
« Little Eva III ». 2nd Fighter Squadron, 52nd Fighter Group.
Pilote: Cpt Varnell. Madna, début 1945.

North American P-51B-15-NA (s/n 42-106750) du 5th
Fighter Squadron, 52nd Fighter Group.
Madna, Italie, juillet 1944.

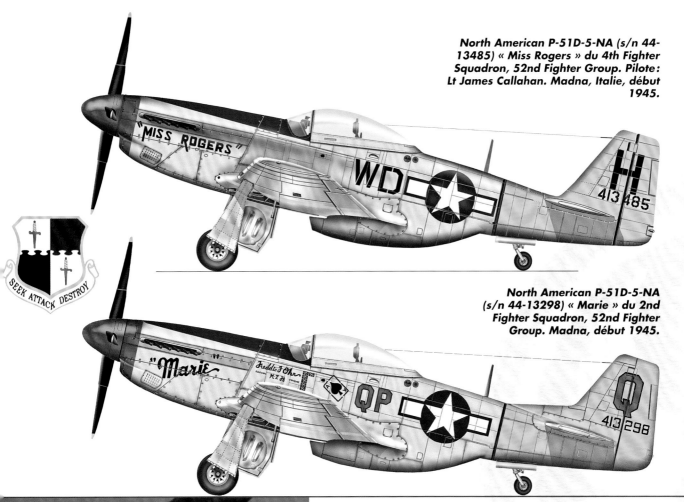

North American P-51D-5-NA (s/n 44-13485) « Miss Rogers » du 4th Fighter Squadron, 52nd Fighter Group. Pilote: Lt James Callahan. Madna, Italie, début 1945.

"MISS ROGERS"

WD ★ H
413485

North American P-51D-5-NA (s/n 44-13298) « Marie » du 2nd Fighter Squadron, 52nd Fighter Group. Madna, début 1945.

"Marie"

QP ★ Q
413298

SEEK ATTACK DESTROY

Major Herschel Green photographed on the wing of his P-51. "Herky" Green was third of the 15th AF aces and was especially the "top scorer" of the "Checkertail Clan" (317th FS, 325th Fighter Group) with 18 confirmed kills (3 on P-40s, 10 on P-47s and 5 on Mustangs), to which must be added ten machines destroyed on the ground. (USAF)

82ND FIGHTER GROUP

The 82nd Fighter Group moved to the airfield at Lecce in Italy in October 1943 and was transferred from the 12th to the 15th Air Force in November, receiving at the same time its P-38 Lightnings. It carried on functioning as a group of fighter-bombers supporting the Allied armies, carrying out interdiction sorties and attacking strategic targets. After receiving two DUCs while operating in the 12th AF, the 82nd Group was awarded a third on 10 June 1944 for having stood up to enemy fighters during a raid on a refinery at Ploesti, Rumania and for destroying chance targets on its way back to base. Its main role was escort, but from October 1943 to May 1945, it also covered the heavy bombers attacking aircraft industry targets, oil refineries in Western and Central Europe as well as the Balkans. The group was deactivated in Italy on 9 September 1945.

The 82nd Fighter Group was made up of three squadrons:

— **95th Fighter Squadron ("Boneheads)**: tactical code "A", distinctive colour: red.

— **96th Fighter Squadron (no nickname)**: tactical code "B", distinctive colour: yellow.

— **97th Fighter Squadron ("Devil-Cats")**: tactical code "C", distinctive colour: blue.

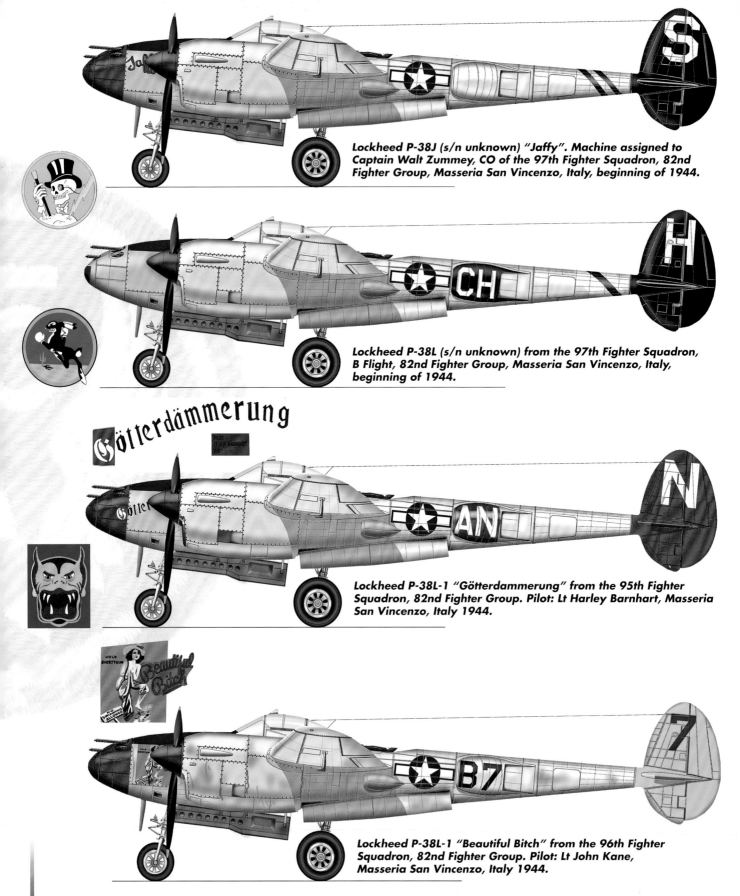

Lockheed P-38J (s/n unknown) "Jaffy". Machine assigned to Captain Walt Zummey, CO of the 97th Fighter Squadron, 82nd Fighter Group, Masseria San Vincenzo, Italy, beginning of 1944.

Lockheed P-38L (s/n unknown) from the 97th Fighter Squadron, B Flight, 82nd Fighter Group, Masseria San Vincenzo, Italy, beginning of 1944.

Lockheed P-38L-1 "Götterdämmerung" from the 95th Fighter Squadron, 82nd Fighter Group. Pilot: Lt Harley Barnhart, Masseria San Vincenzo, Italy 1944.

Lockheed P-38L-1 "Beautiful Bitch" from the 96th Fighter Squadron, 82nd Fighter Group. Pilot: Lt John Kane, Masseria San Vincenzo, Italy 1944.

325TH FIGHTER GROUP

It was on December 1943, that the 325th Fighter Group joined the 15th Air Force on the airfield at Solimane in Tunisia, at the same converting to P-47s. In mid-December, it moved to Foggia, Italy.

Its first mission flying P-47s took place in December 1943 when the group escorted bombers returning from attacking the Axis airfields at Kulamaki, Greece. It was on 30 January 1944 that the most famous P-47 mission in the Mediterranean theatre took place, when Colonel Robert Baseler, the group's CO, led the sixty P-47s preceding the bomber formation. The group, flying at very low altitude over the Adriatic to avoid radar detection, bombed enemy airfields in the Villaorba area in Italy, as well as enemy aircraft taking off to intercept the bombers. In the ensuing dogfight, Major Herky Green alone shot down six planes. The enemy in all lost 28 aircraft against two for the 325th FG. After its first DUC awarded whilst in the 12th AF, the group was awarded a second one for a mission carried out on 30 January 1944 at Villorba.

On 11 March 1944, the 325th Fighter Group shot down ten enemy planes over the Padua marshalling yard in Italy; then on 6 April it claimed another ten over Zagreb airfield, Yugoslavia. Their last mission on P-47s was on 24 May 1944 against the airfield at Wallersdorf, Germany during which six enemy planes were destroyed.

In May 1944, the 325th FG, based at Lesina, Italy converted to P-51s. It carried out escort missions for heavy bombers during long distance attacks on the Messerschmitt works at Regensburg, Germany, as well as the Daimler-Benz armoured vehicles factory in Berlin and the oil refineries in Vienna, Austria. It was at Mondolfo, Italy that the 325th FG ended the war before being sent back to the States in October 1945 to be deactivated.

The 325th Fighter Group, whose marking was a yellow and black checkerboard over the whole tail – hence the nickname "The Checkertail Clan" – was made up of three squadrons:

— **317th Fighter Squadron**: tactical code from 10 to 39, distinctive colour: yellow.
— **318th Fighter Squadron**: tactical code from 40 to 69, distinctive colour: white.
— **319th Fighter Squadron**: tactical code from 70 to 99, distinctive colour: red.

The planes in the headquarters flight (HQ Flight) bore the tactical codes 1 to 9.

Above. **Photographed in flight from his partner's plane, P-47D "Bubble Top" from the 319th FS. The black and yellow checkerboard had been chosen as the emblem by Colonel Baseler, CO of the 325th FG and an admirer of the great German WWI ace, Werner Voss whose habit was to paint his planes thus!**
(USAF)

Republic P-47D (s/n unknown) from the 317th Fighter Squadron, 325th Fighter Group. Pilot: Lt Cecil Dean, Lesina, Italy, April 1944.

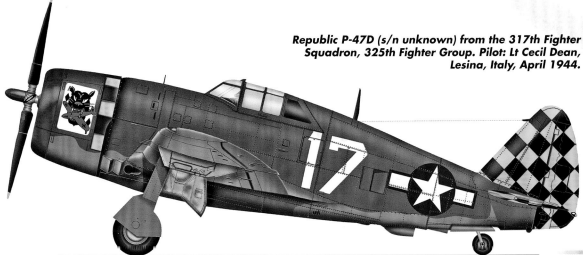

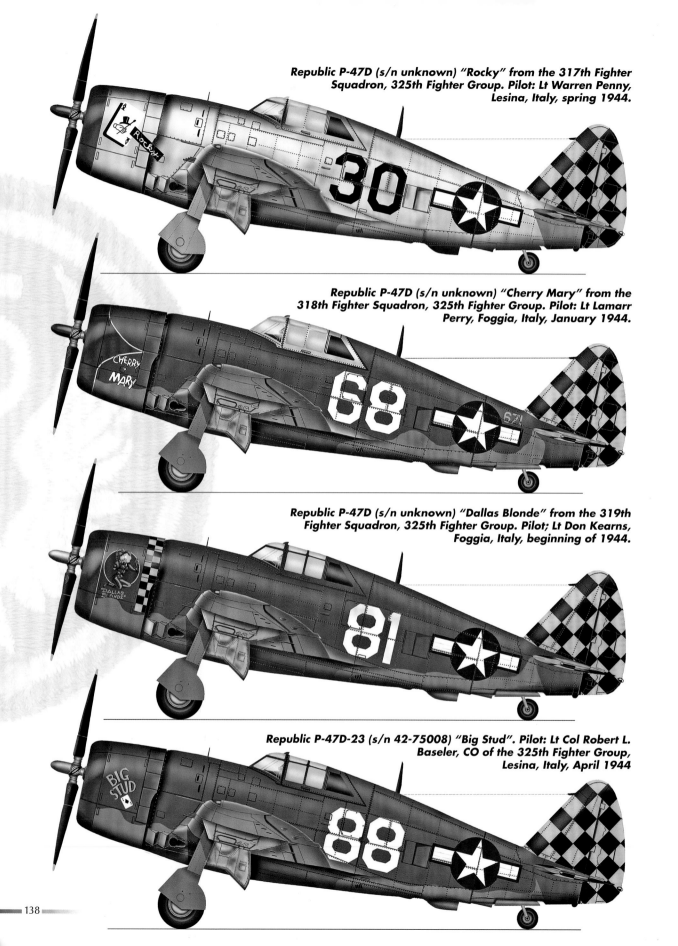

Republic P-47D (s/n unknown) "Rocky" from the 317th Fighter Squadron, 325th Fighter Group. Pilot: Lt Warren Penny, Lesina, Italy, spring 1944.

Republic P-47D (s/n unknown) "Cherry Mary" from the 318th Fighter Squadron, 325th Fighter Group. Pilot: Lt Lamarr Perry, Foggia, Italy, January 1944.

Republic P-47D (s/n unknown) "Dallas Blonde" from the 319th Fighter Squadron, 325th Fighter Group. Pilot; Lt Don Kearns, Foggia, Italy, beginning of 1944.

Republic P-47D-23 (s/n 42-75008) "Big Stud". Pilot: Lt Col Robert L. Baseler, CO of the 325th Fighter Group, Lesina, Italy, April 1944

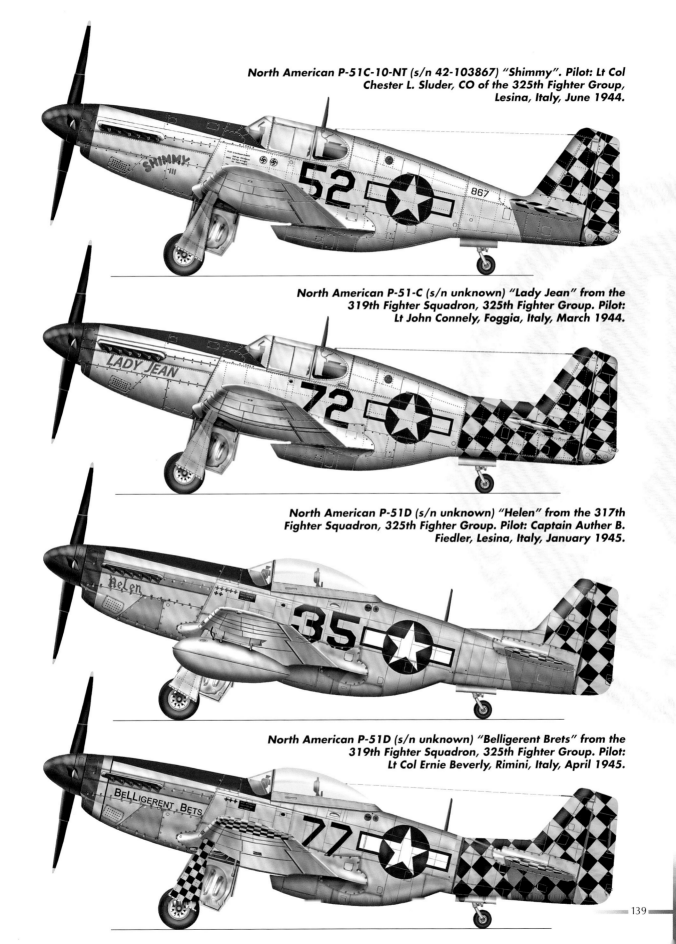

North American P-51C-10-NT (s/n 42-103867) "Shimmy". Pilot: Lt Col Chester L. Sluder, CO of the 325th Fighter Group, Lesina, Italy, June 1944.

North American P-51-C (s/n unknown) "Lady Jean" from the 319th Fighter Squadron, 325th Fighter Group. Pilot: Lt John Connely, Foggia, Italy, March 1944.

North American P-51D (s/n unknown) "Helen" from the 317th Fighter Squadron, 325th Fighter Group. Pilot: Captain Auther B. Fiedler, Lesina, Italy, January 1945.

North American P-51D (s/n unknown) "Belligerent Brets" from the 319th Fighter Squadron, 325th Fighter Group. Pilot: Lt Col Ernie Beverly, Rimini, Italy, April 1945.

332TH FIGHTER GROUP

The 99th Pursuit Squadron, made up on 19 March 1941 and activated on the 22nd, was renamed Fighter Squadron on 15 May 1942. It was made up of Afro-American personnel only who, after training at Tuskegee in Alabama in April 1943, left for Casablanca in Morocco in order to join the 33rd Fighter Group of the 12th Air Force.

The first combat mission of the 99th FG, equipped at the time with P-47s and based at Sebkra Fardjouna, Tunisia, was to attack the Island of Pantelleria in the Mediterranean to free the sea routes and back up the landings in Sicily taking place in July 1943. The 99th was criticised for not having shot down any enemy planes, but it was nonetheless sent to Sicily. It was during the preparations for the landings in Italy that it was awarded a DUC. On 27 and 28 January some Focke-Wulf fighter-bombers carried out a raid on Anzio, Italy where the Allies had landed on 22 January. Attached to the 79th Fighter Group, eleven 99th Fighter Squadron pilots shot down enemy fighters during this raid.

Above. **PFC John T. Fields, the armourer of the 332nd FG is reloading one of his group's Mustangs. In the background is "Stinky II", the P-51C belonging to Captain William J. Stangel of the 328th FS.** *(USAF)*

In February 1944, while equipped with P-39s, the 99th escorted convoys, protected ports and carried out armed reconnaissance missions. It was briefly equipped with P-47s from April to May 1944 then in the following June converted to P-51s.

Three new fighter squadrons, the 100th, 201st and 302nd FS were created after training at Tuskegee and formed the 332nd Fighter Group, made up only of Afro-Americans; they were based at Montecervino, in Italy. The 99th Fighter Squadron was attached to the 332nd Group on 1 May 1944; the group thereby consisted of four squadrons, and was transferred to the 15th Air Force in the same month.

It was from the airfield at Ramitelli on the Italian Adriatic coast that the 332nd Fighter Group escorted the 15th AF's heavy bombers attacking targets in Germany, Austria, Hungary, Poland and Czechoslovakia. During these escort missions, the 332nd FG accumulated a lot of combat records.

The Allied pilots called them the "Red Tails" because of the red tails of the planes - the 332nd FG's mark.

The group was awarded a DUC for a mission carried out on 24 March 1945, escorting B-17s on a raid against the Daimler-Benz armoured vehicles factory in Berlin. On this occasion it encountered Messerschmitt Me-262 jet fighters from the Luftwaffe's JG 7, shooting down seven of them against three P-51s. The unit ended the war based on the airfield at Cattolica on the Italian Adriatic coast and was deactivated on 19 October 1945 after returning to the States.

Bell P-39Q-20 (s/n 44-3028) "Quanto Costa" from the 100th Fighter Squadron, 332nd Fighter Group,

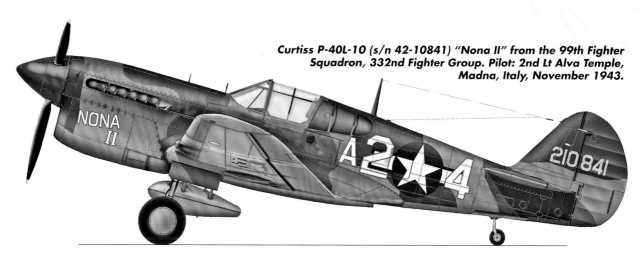

Curtiss P-40L-10 (s/n 42-10841) "Nona II" from the 99th Fighter Squadron, 332nd Fighter Group. Pilot: 2nd Lt Alva Temple, Madna, Italy, November 1943.

Above. **Captain, Andrew D. Turner, CO of the 100th FS getting ready to take off aboard his P-51, in August 1944.** *(USAF)*

Republic P-47D-16 (s/n 42-75971) from the 100th Fighter Squadron, 332nd Fighter Group. Pilot: Lloyd Hathcock, Ramitelli, Italy, May 1944.

Republic P-47D from the 332nd Fighter Group. This plane still bears the markings of its previous posting: insignia and yellow stripe on the tail. Ramitelli, Italy, June 1944.

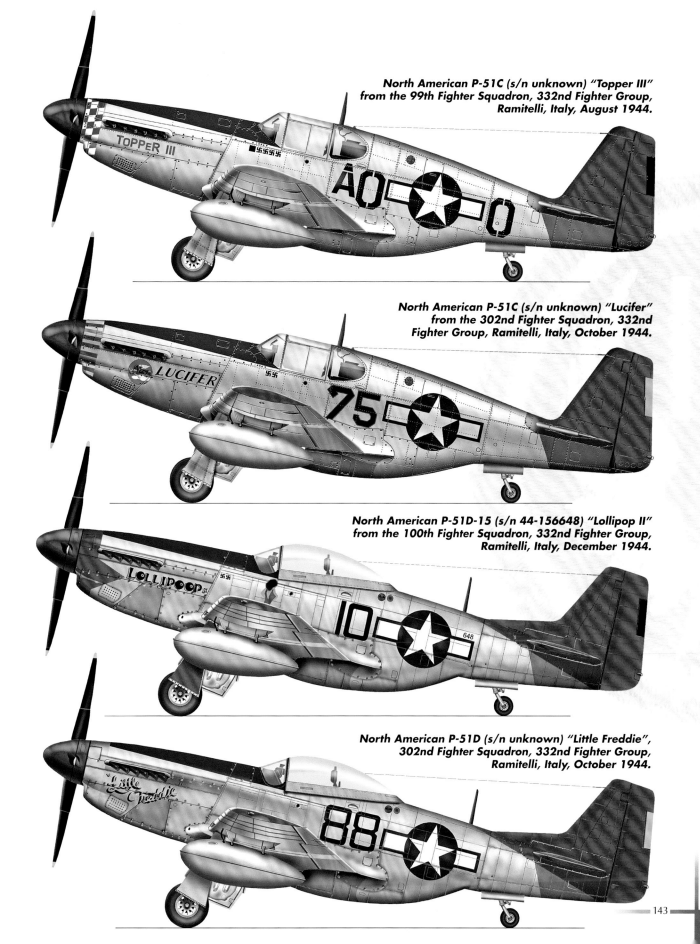

North American P-51C (s/n unknown) "Topper III"
from the 99th Fighter Squadron, 332nd Fighter Group,
Ramitelli, Italy, August 1944.

North American P-51C (s/n unknown) "Lucifer"
from the 302nd Fighter Squadron, 332nd
Fighter Group, Ramitelli, Italy, October 1944.

North American P-51D-15 (s/n 44-156648) "Lollipop II"
from the 100th Fighter Squadron, 332nd Fighter Group,
Ramitelli, Italy, December 1944.

North American P-51D (s/n unknown) "Little Freddie",
302nd Fighter Squadron, 332nd Fighter Group,
Ramitelli, Italy, October 1944.

CONTENTS

12th AIR FORCE

15th AIR FORCE

Translated from the French by Alan McKay

Design and lay-out by Antonin Collet. © *Histoire & Collections 2012*

All rights reserved. No part of this publication can be transmitted or reproduced without a written authority of the autor and the publisher

ISBN: 978-2-35250-210-4

Publisher number; 35250

© *Histoire & Collections 2012*

A book published by
HISTOIRE & COLLECTIONS
SA au capital de 182 938,82 €
5, avenue de la République F-75541 Paris Cedex 11

Tel : +33-1 40 21 18 20/Fax : +33-1 47 00 51 11
www.histoireetcollections.fr

This book has ben designed typed, laid-out and processed by *Histoire & Collections* fully on integrated computer equipment.

Photogravure : *Studio A & C*

Print run completed in March 2012 on the presses of PRINTWORKS INT. Ltd. China.